TREASURE KEEPERS

TREASURE KEEPERS

John FitzMaurice Mills

Aldus Books·Jupiter Books
London

The author wishes to express his gratitude to Dr A. E. Werner, Keeper of the Research Laboratory, British Museum, for his helpful advice and suggestions during the checking of the manuscript.

First published in 1973 by
Aldus Books Limited
Aldus House, 17 Conway Street, London W1P 6BS
and Jupiter Books
167, Hermitige Road, Harringay, London N4 ILZ

© Aldus Books Limited, London 1973
Printed in Spain by Roner, S.A.

SBN 490 00147 5

Contents

Display or Protect?

History, the total story of mankind, comes to life for us when we can see and study the treasures man has left behind in his journey through time. The word "treasure" usually evokes images of jewels and gold and silver plate set with precious stones, or ancient chests bursting with coins, pearls, or uncut diamonds. Yet the smallest finds uncovered on an archaeological dig—a simple stone weapon, some shreds of food left in a tomb a thousand years ago, or the hub and broken spokes of an ancient wheel—all of little intrinsic value

At the Louvre, in Paris, visitors walk freely among these examples of neo-classical sculpture. More fragile—and portable—exhibits are protected by glass cases and controlled lighting.

—may be treasures, too. Treasures of the mind, that is, for each could be a link to man's past, leading to the discovery of new and unexpected wealth of understanding of human history. In this sense, then, the treasure houses of today are the museums and galleries where objects from the past, both workaday articles and the highest expressions of art, give us a fuller picture of the extraordinary mosaic that is our heritage.

The museum or gallery director responsible for such treasures has great responsibility, and must solve numerous problems, none so troublesome as the decision over effective display. He wants the public to see as much as possible, yet at the same time he must protect his highly valuable and often fragile charges.

The perfect way to protect a fading 500-year-old painting or a fragile manuscript dating from 1000 B.C. is not to display it at all, but to hide it away in a light-proof folder locked in a specially made storage cabinet. For the museum visitor, however, this would be total defeat. Some way or other, there has to be a compromise, a safety limit that will allow inspection without bringing destruction to the exhibit. For instance, at London's National Gallery, a drawing by Leonardo da Vinci is kept under a low level of illumination because light tends to fade what remains of the fragile work. Ideally, it should be kept in total darkness, but this would destroy its value as a work of art—no one could see it.

Light, strangely enough, is one of the greatest of museum hazards. Actually it is not visible light, but the invisible ultraviolet rays in sunlight and artificial illumination that can damage pigments and dyes, textile fibers (both natural and synthetic), gums and glues, varnishes, and even paper. The effect of sunlight on the media of oil paintings is less certain, but it will cause the varnish on them to discolor, crack, and decompose. Watercolor paintings are even more easily affected, because their pigments are not protected by a skin of dried oil.

Uncontrolled light will fade the rich colors of embroideries and tapestries in a matter of weeks. Fading is not the only danger: under certain light conditions, the fibers actually disintegrate. This happens when their molecular structure breaks down as the result of chemical reactions caused by ultraviolet light. Over a period of years, for example, exposure to light can turn beautiful silk garments to fine dust. So, for many objects, dim lighting is one answer to the conflicting demands of display and protection.

Before the quantity of light can be controlled, it has to be measured. The international unit for measuring light is the *lux,* the amount of illumination falling on a surface placed one meter from a light source of standard brilliance, known as the *international candle.* On a bright summer's day in England or the United States a surface exposed to direct sunlight can register as high as 100,000 lux. On a gray, heavily overcast day, the inside walls of a gallery or museum will probably register around 600 lux. Curators of paintings generally agree that a maximum of 150 lux is best for oil paintings. For particularly sensitive exhibits such as watercolors, prints, drawings, and tapestries the recommended level drops to 50 lux, which still permits adequate viewing.

Today more and more art museums exclude natural light

Dim light permits visitors at London's National Gallery to see Leonardo da Vinci's drawing of *The Virgin and Saint Anne with the Christ Child*, but keeps the inevitable fading to a minimum.

altogether in favor of artificial light, which is much easier to regulate. Those that still depend on daylight often take elaborate steps to keep its intensity at recommended levels. At the Victoria and Albert Museum in London, for example, the Royal collection of tapestries and drawings is protected with a system of electronically operated Venetian blinds on windows and skylights. Variations in daylight intensity are detected by photocells that control the electrical circuits supplying power to motors that open and close the blinds.

Another way of controlling light is to block out the damaging ultraviolet radiation. Special glass made by laminating two layers of clear glass with a central layer of ultraviolet absorbing plastic is widely used for glazing paintings and for building display cases. A much less expensive technique is to coat ordinary glass with a type of varnish that partly absorbs the ultraviolet.

Although low-intensity illumination is by far the most effective protection for light-sensitive exhibits, it can be unpleasant for museum goers. Museum officials know this, and throughout the world the search goes on for a workable compromise between the need to protect and the need to display. Architects and designers are working with museum officials to plan museum displays so that there is a balance

Three centuries of air pollution have eroded and darkened these statues of saints on St. Paul's Cathedral, in London.

Modern display techniques at the Victoria and Albert Museum in London show these medieval treasures to best advantage, and protect them from accidental damage, vandalism, and theft.

between viewing and protecting and so that transitions from normally lit areas to areas of controlled light are neither too abrupt nor too frequent.

Next to light, or perhaps on a par with it as a destroyer of man's treasures, comes polluted air. As our world becomes increasingly industrialized, vast amounts of corrosive gases and other harmful substances are poured into the atmosphere. Of all these, the most potentially dangerous substance is sulfur dioxide gas; millions of tons of it are produced each year. In Los Angeles, cars and trucks belch out some 400 tons of it every day. Each year, in every major city coal fires and oil-burning furnaces release sulfur dioxide by the tens of thousands of tons.

When sulfur dioxide dissolves in rain, snow, or fog it turns into sulfuric acid. This highly corrosive acid attacks stone and metal surfaces, the mellowed polish of old furniture, unpro-

tected paintings, and, in fact, most museum objects. The attack may be quick and dramatic, or in other cases, the destructive agents in the environment may go about their job with slow but grim efficiency. Over the years canvas fibers are weakened, colors fade, surfaces corrode and crumble. Examination of stone carvings and metalwork close to some chemical manufacturing complex or huge smoke-belching plant, tells the story all too clearly. Staining, surface etching, and crumbling can be found everywhere. Even buildings and sculpture erected in the 20th century are threatened, for noticeable deterioration can be seen in even a few years.

Industrial air pollution, however, is not the only hazard. In desert climates, such as in North Africa, the Middle East, and the American Southwest, dust, sand, and excessive dryness are the main dangers. In damp tropical climates excess humidity makes for problems by favoring the growth of molds that can cause discoloring and rot. Museums in coastal areas are threatened by salt that blows in on the sea winds.

Every museum needs a system of air filtration. It is possible to set up equipment that will remove up to 99 per cent of fine dust from incoming air, but the cost is enormous and such high-performance equipment is unnecessary in museums. More practical units operate at about 95 per cent efficiency, but even these are beyond the resources of most museums. Because sulfur dioxide is very easily dissolved in water, most of this harmful gas can be removed by washing the incoming air—simply by passing it through a water spray. Another method is to pass the air over a bed of charcoal treated to increase its absorbing capacity. Although this does not remove much more than 60 per cent of the gas on the first pass, recirculation improves the result.

While filtration is the answer to air pollution, air conditioning is the way to control the amount of moisture in the air. Moisture content is measured in terms of *relative humidity*. For the majority of exhibits, the ideal relative humidity reading is between 50 and 65 per cent. When the relative humidity is too low, paper, leather, and wood can become brittle, sometimes dangerously so. If it is too high, especially if the ventilation is bad and rooms become damp, mold growths may start and rotting takes place.

In dry climates the relative humidity can be raised by equipment that will evaporate water vapor into the air by the use of an atomizing spray in the incoming air ducts. Where the climate is naturally damp, incoming air can be made dryer by air conditioning equipment, or it can be drawn through a water absorbent substance.

While struggling with the problems of light control and air conditioning, the often harried director must always keep in mind the other side of the problem: displaying his exhibits to their best advantage. In the past, when it sometimes seemed that the prime objective of museums was to collect as many items as possible without regard for exhibition, heavy, cumbersome cases often dwarfed the objects on display. Visitors could easily become confused and wander in aimless frustration among unimaginative arrays of cluttered cases, unable to find what they were looking for or see the relationships among displayed items.

In present-day museum practice, the design of a new display is approached much in the way a film script is visualized for television or cinema. The film producer knows that to maintain interest he has to punctuate his story by visual change. He uses cuts, dissolves, and shots from different angles and distances to give visual excitement to his film. In many museums, a near parallel treatment has been adopted. Good lettering and exciting graphic displays that inform and also whet the appetite lead to exhibits imaginatively arranged to provide a wide variety of viewing angles.

Ultimately, what is important is the imagination and creativity of the designers. On the whole, people who go to museums are looking for information, for entertainment, or for a mixture of both. Whether an exhibit is an early industrial machine, a tapestry woven in the Middle Ages, or a fragment of Roman mosaic flooring, its value to the visitor is partly determined by the way in which it is displayed.

The British Museum in London has made dramatic use of light to display the unusual properties of a remarkably fine piece of late Roman glass, dating from the fourth to fifth century A.D. and known as the "Lycurgus Cup." When it is lit from the front, the opaque green color of the glass makes the figures and the exquisite decoration stand out in bold relief. If an alternative light source from behind is arranged, a hitherto unsuspected quality in the glass is brought out. Quite suddenly, the opaque green color disappears, and the transmitted light brings out a rich translucent ruby and amethyst color. Glass that appears to have one color in reflected light and another in transmitted light is called "dichroic."

Closed-circuit television helps guard exhibits in Coventry's Herbert Art Gallery and Museum against vandals and thieves. The monitor attendant can communicate with guards in the exhibit area by push-button telephone.

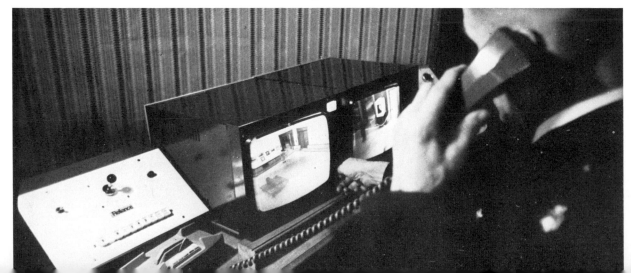

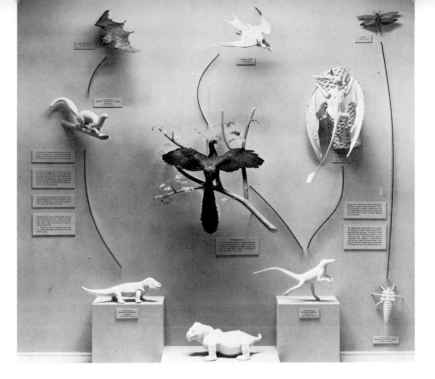

New-style display cases sometimes tell a story rather than just line up the exhibits in a formal manner. Here is an example illustrating flight in nature, which is both imaginative and decorative.

Today the designers of museum exhibit cases work with a wide range of transparent plastic materials. One of the most important materials is a clear plastic, called *Lucite* or *Perspex*. Sheets of this plastic can be joined, either self-to-self or by thin frames, to make cases elegant in appearance as well as strong and long lasting. Lucite sheets are nearly shatterproof, and an alarm system of fine wires can easily be cast into them to add extra protection.

The wealth of modern synthetic materials has also made mounting and presenting exhibits a much easier job. Wood, one of the most popular materials of the past, is still widely used, but it has a number of serious disadvantages. The tendency of wood to shrink or expand with even very small variations in relative humidity can easily damage an exhibit. For example, the expansion of a wooden mount for a fragile headdress could break it open.

Although Lucite is ideal for building strong frames and supports it cannot easily be molded into three-dimensional shapes. Better suited for this job is another synthetic resin, *polyurethane,* a type of casting material that comes as a dry powder and reacts with a chemical known as a hardener to form a lightweight solid. A museum worker, using polyurethane to form a model head to display a helmet or mask, first makes a plaster mold of the object and fills it with the resin in its dry form. Once he adds the hardener, the model head sets up hard. Then the mold can be broken away to leave the model head ready for the display case. Another advantage of the polyurethane is that it is comparatively easy to carve; usually only the main outlines of the face are modeled, for too much detail would distract attention from the exhibit itself.

While attracting visitors to displays, the museum must also protect the displays from the visitors. The museum director knows that at every hour of the day and night there is the possibility of theft. Unfortunately he also knows that in the crowds that throng the galleries may lurk the "collector" thieves who take a fancy to an unguarded exhibit and then take it. Just as dangerous is the vandal who may do damage just for a kick. Armed with a ball-point pen he may poke out the eyes of a portrait, pick a lump of paint off a Van Gogh landscape or carve his initials on an ancient marble.

On the night of September 14, 1959, six works, including paintings by Rembrandt, Frans Hals, Rubens, and Renoir, valued at $700,000, vanished from the Toronto Art Gallery. About three weeks later police were tipped off that the paintings were hidden in a garage near the gallery. They found them there, largely unharmed, but were never able to track down the thieves.

Two years later, one of the finest collections of modern art in France vanished overnight. Art thieves had broken all records by stealing 57 paintings in a single raid from the Annonciade Museum in Saint-Tropez. When cleaners opened the museum on the morning after the raid, they found the walls of the ground floor gallery completely bare. About half of the entire collection was gone. The only encouraging point about this remarkable robbery is that the museum eventually recovered all but one of the paintings.

Objects from a royal ancestor altar of the Kingdom of Benin (in what is now Nigeria) are displayed on a stepped platform suggesting the altar from which they were taken. The warm red background—used throughout the room—heightens the dramatic impact of a large collection of African art objects. The room is part of the British Museum's Department of Ethnography.

One summer afternoon in 1960 the famous Uffizi Gallery in Florence, Italy, was crowded with tourists and Florentines enjoying the famous collection of Renaissance paintings. Suddenly, to the astonishment of a group of people standing around a biblical painting by Giovanni Morandi, a 17th-century Italian artist, the picture crashed to the floor. Two attendants rushed forward. When they lifted the painting to examine it, they noticed some writing scrawled on the back of the canvas. "Thank you," it said, "I have always liked Morandi." Underneath was a date, several weeks earlier. The impertinent thief had painted—or commissioned someone else to paint—a copy that had fooled both the museum-goers and attendants for weeks.

Oddly enough, there is at least one instance in which stolen art has been held as a kind of political hostage. On March 22, 1971, the newspapers of Florence reported an art raid by the "Doomwatch gang." The report said that 10 days previously two valuable paintings had vanished from the Palazzo Vecchio in the city. They were *Madonna and Child* by Masaccio, a painter of the Florentine School, and *Portrait of a Gentleman* by Hans Memling, the Flemish painter. The Florence city council offered a $15,000 reward for their return. On the following day, the police and leading Italian newspapers received a letter signed the "Doomwatch Guerillas." The thieves wrote, "We stole the paintings as a protest against officialdom's inefficiency in fighting pollution." The "Guerillas" further stated that the paintings were "safe and in good hands—at least for now." The letter went on, "Local authorities issue orders against pollution, but do nothing about having them enforced. . . . When one factory in each of the 10 main (North Italian) cities has been truly shut down we will return the paintings." In this case conscience gained the upper hand. Having made their point, the Doomwatch gang returned the paintings safely.

How can robberies like those just mentioned take place? It is a sad fact that the growing number of thefts constantly reflect inadequacies in museum buildings and security systems. In the United States alone about five or six museum or gallery exhibits are stolen each day, and not only paintings. Statues, books, and curios attract not only the professional art thief, but the light-fingered amateur collector as well. Small statuettes, glass paperweights, watches, pistols have often vanished from museums, no doubt into the large pocket of an art thief who has more in common with the shoplifter than the master criminal.

As more and more people take to collecting, either for its own sake or as an investment, the value of every work of art is soaring, that of antiquities most particularly. And the prices collectors will pay for paintings appear to be rising out of all reason. In 1970 a Van Gogh *Les Cypres et l'arbre en Fleurs* was

A seemingly "magical" transformation occurs in the Lycurgus Cup, a late-Roman glass vessel, when its light source is changed. Lit from the front (*top*), it appears opaque and greenish in color. When light is transmitted from within the cup (*below*), it becomes translucent and ruby-red.

sold for $1,300,000. But in the same year, a new world record price for a single painting went to a work of a 17th-century Spanish artist, Diego Velázquez, when his portrait of *Juan de Pareja* sold for $5,544,000. At first glance it is not surprising that thieves are more and more attracted to museums and art galleries. What is so puzzling, however, is how they can hope to dispose of well-known and often well-documented articles. Sometimes stolen pictures or other objects turn up in unlikely places, such as lockers in railway stations, pointing perhaps to a baffled thief who, once he has got possession of the rich property, realizes he cannot dispose of it. But a significant number vanish forever—sometimes into the collections of rich eccentrics for their own private enjoyment.

Security systems are under pressure, and the job of security officers is made ever more difficult by the vast number of museum and gallery visitors. Surveys show that each year more than 22 million people visit 12,000 establishments throughout the world.

The simpler means of protecting exhibits include, in addition to ever-vigilant guards, such devices as armor plating, pick-proof locks, and unbreakable glass; but the most determined criminals can deal with these security aids. More costly, but more effective, are new electronic systems that use a whole range of techniques, from television scanning to ultrasonic alarm beams.

Television cameras, radar scanners, and infrared detectors are also used to transmit images to a central observation room where guards constantly keep exhibits in view day and night. Special microphones, tuned to ignore all normal sound but to respond to the noise of tools, such as saws or drills, are also in

Above: Packing the *Pieta*. Tiny beads of expanded polystyrene cushion the priceless marble statue, here being prepared for its transatlantic journey to the 1964 New York World's Fair. The cushioning material also made the crate buoyant, so that it would float in the event of a shipwreck.

Moving exhibits in the museum always calls for the maximum care, as even a massive and seemingly indestructible object such as this Aztec head can easily become damaged.

use. Instruments that give out a continuous ultrasonic beam are placed in galleries so that, if a would-be thief walks through, the beam is cut and alarms are triggered. Ordinary light beams and infrared beams are used in a similar way. Another security system uses heat-sensitive detectors placed in such a way that a blowtorch or even the heat generated by a drill will activate an electronic device, causing it to set off any one of a number of alarms. One drastic kind detonates an explosive charge that can stun the thief or throw him into a state of panic. This last, of course, can only be used in a part of the museum away from exhibits.

One security system in Vienna relies on an elaborate system of 30 signals. Guards patrolling the building must trigger these signals according to a fixed time schedule. If any guard fails to report at a signal point, all museum exits are automatically barred, and police are alerted by a direct cable link. So acute is the security problem that this museum does not want its name known, nor will it provide any details of its system.

There are many more security devices used by museums and galleries that can afford them. But as in every aspect of museum maintenance and operation, protection hinges on the question of money, and good security systems are not cheap. Effective but intricate security is so expensive to run that it can be used only to protect the most precious exhibits. For example, the Louvre, in Paris, is protected with an alarm system that costs more than $45,000 to install.

When it comes to spending the limited amount of money available for the upkeep of museums, local governments are often faced with a problem of priorities. Given a limited budget, should it be spent on making museums comfortable

Safe at home in the Louvre, after a two-month visit to the United States in 1963, the *Mona Lisa* is carefully removed from its special container. Blocks of spongy plastic on each side of the painting kept it from touching the container's inner surface.

for visitors or on protecting exhibits from both thieves and the environment? Usually the need to attract visitors is seen as the higher priority. But as one museum security officer has said, "Security expensive . . .? Not the morning after!"

Money, however, is not the only problem. Many of the most effective but obviously unpopular security measures obstruct visitors in one way or another. Limiting the number of people in a gallery at one time, for instance, would certainly make it easier to keep an eye on things, but it would never be acceptable to display-conscious boards of directors or public officials. A compromise must be found, and, even in museums that can afford to spend tens of thousands of dollars on security, calculated risks must be taken.

One such risk a museum often accepts is to allow an exhibit to go on tour and thus expose it to the not always predictable dangers of travel. Not everyone has the chance or the money to go abroad to see the national treasures of other lands, and for this reason cultural organizations repeatedly request museum administrators to allow unique works of art to be shown in their countries. Fortunately, there have been remarkably few instances of major loss or damage, but the possibility is always there.

How far are the custodians of irreplaceable works of art justified in exposing them to the risks of a long journey? Clearly, it would be best if precious works never left their permanent homes. There, at least, they can be constantly observed and cared for by trained personnel under controlled conditions. In the past, exchanges between museums and galleries did take place, but in a limited way. Most often, however, works were sent no farther than from one European country to another, usually within a region of fairly similar climate. The trend nowadays, however, is toward more and more wide-ranging traveling exhibitions. It is unlikely that it will ever be reversed, and since the early 1950s, journeys from a temperate area through the tropics to a cold area have become commonplace as museums have begun to send exhibits all over the world.

When precious objects pass through regions of widely different relative humidities and temperatures, condensation can easily form in their containers, a situation that can quickly lead to mold growths on paintings or corrosion on metals. A bronze statue of Buddha was damaged in this way when it was sent from Japan for exhibition in the United States. As the ship carrying the statue passed from a warm area through a cold one and into another warm one again, condensation formed and a mild surface corrosion destroyed much of the statue's patina.

Expert opinion is that any container designed for transporting treasures of art or antiquity should be thoroughly

Opposite: This portrait of *Juan de Pareja* by Velázquez made news in the art world when it was knocked down for a seven-figure sum.
Below: The scene at Christie's in London during the sale of the record-breaking Velázquez. In a few short, tense minutes another price peak was passed.

airtight. To hold the relative humidity at safe levels, quantities of specially treated wood or hydroscopic (water-absorbing) material must be added to the container's packing to soak up and retain moisture. Provided that the amount of absorbent materials is correct, the relative humidity will be kept constant. Too little, and it may rise; too much, and it may fall. Keeping the temperature steady is easier. The case is simply lined with a layer of insulating material.

Besides the steps taken to control the container's temperature and humidity, cushioning material is needed as a safeguard against anything from a sudden bump to the often not-too-gentle vibration caused by aircraft or ship engines. A work of ceramic or marble is especially vulnerable, for even fairly gentle vibration, if constant, can cause tiny cracks to form inside that will weaken and eventually damage its whole structure.

In 1962, Pope John XXIII authorized the transportation of Michelangelo's *Pietà* from the Vatican to the 1964-65 New York World's Fair. The major problem of packing this most famous of marble statues was to ensure complete protection from even the most minute vibration. After numerous painstaking tests, it was decided to bury the statue in beads of expanded plastic foam inside two huge packing cases. The inner case of wood held the statue cushioned in literally millions of the tiny plastic globes. The outer one was of steel. Both cases were lined with slabs of resilient plastic as further

insulation. And as an added safety, the packing case was mounted on the ship's deck in a place that was least likely to be affected by vibration from its engines. A footnote to the operation was that if the ship carrying the *Pietà* had foundered on its way to New York, the packing case, despite a weight of about five tons, would still have floated. Although no one expected the ship to sink, the case was fitted with a special transmitter designed to send out automatically an international distress signal if the need arose.

Despite the careful planning, the Vatican art curators knew that the only real test of their work was the journey itself. The operation went without snags, and the *Pietà* was eventually returned safely to the Vatican. Was the risk justified? No one can say, but 27 million visitors at New York's World's Fair had seen and admired Michelangelo's great masterpiece.

Ironically, while "safely" at home in St. Peter's, in May 1972, the *Pietà* was savagely attacked by a lunatic who claimed to be Jesus Christ. Sadly, this happened just one month before the famous work of art was due to be enclosed by unbreakable glass, a step the Vatican officials had already planned. Wielding a hammer, the man leaped upon the statue and struck it several blows, damaging it severely before he was stopped. It took restorers nearly a year to repair the damage, using a marble paste. The *Pietà* was then returned to its place in St. Peter's—now protected by bullet-proof glass and an alarm system.

Also in 1962, the *Mona Lisa* left its permanent home in the Louvre, the great museum in Paris, and traveled by sea to be exhibited in Washington, D.C., and, later, in New York. The problems in planning the journey were similar to those involved in transporting the *Pietà,* but paintings are far more sensitive to changes in temperature and humidity than are marble statues. The reluctance of the Louvre authorities to send the *Mona Lisa* on a several months' tour of the United States can be easily understood. They had to ask themselves what their responsibilities were, not only toward the painting, but toward their museum, their country, and toward the rest of the world. Eventually they did allow the trip. Even so, despite elaborate precautions, many voices were raised in protest.

In the Louvre, the *Mona Lisa,* which is painted on a wooden panel and not canvas, is kept in 50 per cent relative humidity at a temperature of 64°F. For its transatlantic voyage, the Louvre experts ordered an airtight container insulated with six-inch-thick sheets of a type of plastic known as polyvinyl chloride (PVC). They chose PVC not only because it acts as an efficient insulator, but also because it is extremely shock-absorbent. The painting itself was held in position in the container by fitted blocks of spongy plastic, similar to that used to make cups for hot drinks. Finally, it was sealed with pieces of rubber at top and bottom.

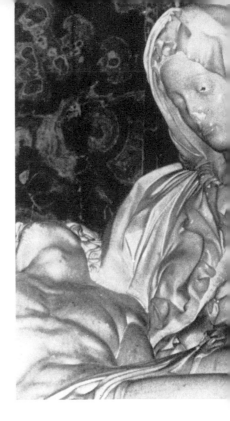

Right: A bystander's camera caught this picture of Laszlo Toth attacking the *Pieta* in St. Peter's, Rome, in May, 1972.
Above: Some of the damage done by Toth before he was pulled away from the statue. The Virgin's nose and left eye are chipped, and the left arm has been severed at the elbow.

To make sure that the container would protect its precious contents, it was first tested with a far less valuable wood panel painting of approximately the same age as the *Mona Lisa*. The technicians in charge sealed instruments alongside it to measure and record temperature and relative humidity. Then they placed the container in an *environmental chamber,* a device that can, practically at the touch of a button, simulate any desired climate with appropriate temperature and relative humidity. By adjusting conditions inside the chamber, the technicians sent the container on an imaginary journey through several different climatic regions. When the container was opened, the Louvre shipping specialists found that the design had proved effective—temperature and relative humidity inside had remained constant throughout all the external variations.

Apart from the precautions in packing the painting, elaborate security measures were taken during the real journey of the priceless *Mona Lisa*. Throughout the trip and exhibition in the United States, the *Mona Lisa* was watched day and night by armed guards. Only a limited number of people were allowed into the viewing halls at one time.

Three months after it had left the Louvre, the *Mona Lisa* had returned. More than $1\frac{1}{2}$ million people from all over the United States had seen the painting. The museum authorities had shown considerable courage in agreeing to the operation in the first place. Technicians had proved their ability to protect a delicate and irreplaceable masterpiece even through the rigors of a 6,000-mile round trip ocean voyage.

The Investigators

In many ways the most important of the 20th-century additions to museums and galleries is a laboratory, where new acquisitions can be given detailed scrutiny, and where exhibits showing signs of damage can be brought for diagnosis and treatment.

The first museum laboratory was opened in 1883, in what was then the *Staatliche Museen* in Berlin. But this pioneer laboratory no longer exists.

The museum laboratory movement got its real start when after World War I, a small laboratory was opened at the British Museum in London. Originally intended as a temporary arrangement to repair the deterioration suffered by the museum's collections that had been stored in the city's subway system away from the threat of German bombs, the laboratory has grown in size and importance and today occupies a complete building. In 50 years of continual existence, the British Museum Research Laboratory has dealt with almost every type of object except easel paintings.

Other museums and art galleries soon followed suit. The Louvre opened its laboratory in 1925; the Museum of Fine Arts, Boston, in 1927; and the New York Metropolitan Museum of Art in 1930. The next stage in the development was the appearance of independent laboratories devoted to the conservation of works of art, but not necessarily associated with any particular museum or gallery. Two laboratories of this type are the *Institut Royal du Patrimoine Artistique* (roughly the Royal Institute of Artistic Heritage) in Brussels, set up in 1938, and the *Instituto Centrale del Restauro* established in Rome under the auspices of UNESCO in 1959. Today most newly built museums and galleries endeavor to include at least one room for examination and conservation work and some have large, elaborately equipped laboratories.

The first task of the scientists who work in these laboratories is to find out what an object is made of, how and where it was made, and to make sure it is not a copy or fake. A second and equally important task is to use scientific methods and technology to repair and restore the museum's treasures. Repair and restoration may be needed when an object is first brought into the museum, or to salvage an exhibit damaged by the hazards of display.

A typical example of museum laboratory work might go like this: A metal figure, supposedly a Roman bronze, might be brought in for an opinion as to its origin and likely authenticity. The laboratory technician, using his knowledge of chemistry and metals, analyzes the figure and, let us assume, discovers it is not bronze at all, but almost pure zinc. At this point the chemist has done his job, but his report provides information to evaluate the figure. The experts now know that it is not Roman, because pure zinc was not available in Roman times, and is probably a recently made fake.

Knowing where ores with certain impurities are mined can play a vital part in the scientific detective work, but traces of impurities in ancient metals cannot always be linked with known ore deposits. First, metal objects are often made by remelting scrap metal that may have come from many different areas. Secondly, some of the deposits worked centuries ago may now be exhausted and unknown to modern scientists.

A chemist frequently faced with ancient metal mixtures, or alloys, might find it useful to examine just how much the craftsmen of olden times knew about controlling their composition. Take as an example bronze, an alloy of copper and tin. Bronze made today contains about 90 per cent copper and rarely more than 9 or 10 per cent tin. Many ancient bronzes, however, had a tin content ranging from about 2 per cent to 16 per cent.

From the 18th Dynasty (1570-1300 B.C.) onward in ancient Egypt, bronze was extensively used for casting small statuettes. When scientists in the early 1960s examined some of these small figures they found sharp variations in the composition of the bronze. Obviously, the early Egyptian metalsmiths either had many formulas for mixing the tin and copper or they made no effort to control the production of the alloy. It is interesting, however, to note that when a similar investigation was made of examples of Greek and Roman bronze statues, results showed a much stricter control in the manufacture of bronze. This analysis also brought out the fact that the Greek bronze contains practically no lead, but does have a relatively high proportion of tin compared with Roman bronze, which has a small proportion of tin and a moderately high proportion of lead. By using the analyses of metal objects of known antiquity as a guideline, chemists may often help in the dating of a new find or turn up a copy or a fake.

The composition of ancient glass has also provided the analyst with a few surprises. Hundreds of ancient glass objects from different periods and civilizations have been analyzed, including examples from Egypt, the Far and Near East, the Roman Empire, India, Medieval and Renaissance Europe, and Russia. The results of the scientists' work make it clear that craftsmen in different parts of the world and at different times

This figure, allegedly a Roman bronze, was found to be made of pure zinc when analyzed by emission spectrography.

Above: An X-ray photograph of Raphael's portrait of Pope Julius II *(below)*. Long considered to be a copy, the painting was subjected to tests that proved it was the original. The X ray revealed experiments and changes by the artist that would probably not have been painted by someone making a copy. Analysis of the paint itself showed the use of walnut oil as a medium—a characteristic of Raphael's work.

must have added special ingredients that would affect the transparency, the color, and the working properties of the glass.

One such series of tests was run on more than 200 specially chosen samples of clear glass from the Middle East, North Africa, and Europe, dating from the 5th century B.C. to the 12th century A.D. This systematic study soon showed scientists that the composition of early glass fell into definite categories. Roman glass from the sixth century B.C. to the fourth century A.D. was rich in antimony, but from the fourth century A.D. to the ninth century it was low in antimony and rich in manganese. Early Islamic (Egyptian, Syrian, Mesopotamian, and Persian) glass from the eighth century A.D. to the tenth century had neither antimony nor manganese but was high in potassium and magnesium.

When a chemist sets out to identify the kinds of elements that are present in any given object he first uses the technique of *qualitative chemical analysis*. Once he knows what elements are present in an object, he can then employ *quantitative methods of analysis* to determine the actual proportions in which the different elements are present. In most cases, however, museum scientists can only hope to obtain very small samples from a valuable object, so they use a technique known as *microchemical analysis*. These sensitive methods give

In the Louvre laboratory, a bronze sphinx is analyzed by a physicist using spectrography. On being subjected to high frequency rays, the statue emits radiations characteristic of the metals it contains. In this case, the presence of an alloy of copper, pewter, and lead was detected.

A fragment of the Dead Sea Scrolls photographed *(top)* under ordinary light and *(bottom)* under infrared radiation.

precise results from tiny samples and have greatly expanded the range of problems that can be worked on.

In the collection of the Uffizi Gallery in Florence, Italy, there is a portrait of Pope Julius II that had long been regarded as an original work of the great Italian painter, Raphael. In 1970 the authenticity of the portrait came under suspicion, and the curators of the Uffizi recataloged the painting as being "after Raphael," meaning a painting done in his style, possibly even by a student. Another version of the painting, regarded merely as a good copy of the Uffizi original, had been in the reserve collection of London's National Gallery for some 140 years. It was an interesting but not important example of Renaissance painting, worth a few thousand dollars. News of the Uffizi's reclassification gave the authorities in the London gallery a jolt, and caused them to take another look at their portrait of Julius.

Among the analytical chemical techniques used on the portrait was one that could identify the kind of oil the artist had used to make up his paints. The exciting discovery was that the medium to make up the paint used in two parts of the picture was not linseed oil—which was commonly used by artists in the 1500s—but walnut oil. The art historians knew that Raphael was one of the few painters of that time to favor walnut oil as a medium. This, together with X-ray evidence showing experimental changes very much in the style of Raphael made by the artist and later painted over, convinced the art world that the National Gallery had indeed the original Raphael portrait of Pope Julius II. Almost overnight the painting became worth several million dollars

A number of important techniques now in fairly common use in museum laboratories rely on the physical properties of different kinds of radiations such as X rays, gamma rays, and ultraviolet and infrared radiation. One of these techniques, *X-ray diffraction analysis,* is especially important in identifying crystalline materials, since each crystalline material gives a unique characteristic pattern, called a diffraction pattern. Thus each crystalline material gives its own "fingerprint" as it were.

Over the years thousands of X-ray diffraction analyses on known compounds have provided scientists with a catalog of patterns. This technique can be used for identifying corrosion products on metal, for determining the nature of the different semiprecious stones used to make cylinder seals.

X-ray diffraction analysis has also been used to identify the material that the ancient peoples used as the opacifying agent in the production of their opaque or translucent glasses. These materials are generally crystalline, dispersed in the glass matrix which is noncrystalline. It follows, then, that the X-ray diffraction pattern given by a sample of opaque glass will be characteristic of the crystalline substance it contains. This

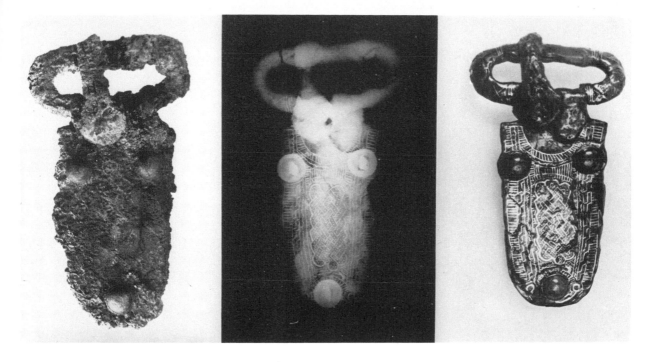

This buckle, dating from the Dark Ages, was so covered with rust when it was found in Belgium in 1908 that cleaning it seemed a hopeless and unprofitable undertaking. An X-ray photo *(center)* taken in 1955 revealed the true state of the iron base and silver decoration, and indicated that restoration was possible. The photo at right shows the buckle after cleaning.

method has shown that in the white and blue opaque glasses of the Egyptian and Roman periods up to the fourth century A.D. calcium antimonate was present as an opacifying agent, whereas from the fifth century A.D. onward this was replaced by tin oxide. Modern glassmakers generally use calcium fluoride for this purpose. However, a study of Chinese opaque, so-called "jade," glass brought to light the interesting fact that in the T'ang period (A.D. 618-907) calcium fluoride was being used as an opacifying agent in glass a thousand years before it was used in the West.

E mission spectroscopy, another technique in common use in the museum laboratory, is based on the principle that when a substance is heated to the glowing point in an electric arc, it emits light consisting of particular wavelengths, depending upon the elements present. When this light is passed through a prism in the spectroscope it is split up into its constituent wavelengths. And, just as in the case of the diffraction patterns of crystals, each chemical element produces a characteristic spectrum. By comparing the light emitted by a sample with spectra from known elements, the scientist can tell what elements are present in the sample.

There may be some cases in which the museum scientists cannot obtain a sample for analysis. For instance, not even the smallest piece of a metal coin or a small precious porcelain object can be removed for tests. To analyze objects like these the scientist will turn to one or another of the modern non-destructive techniques, such as *X-ray fluorescence spectroscopy* or *electron-beam analysis.*

X-ray fluorescence spectroscopy depends on the fact that, if an object is bombarded with a primary beam of X rays, a characteristic beam of secondary X rays—i.e., the so-called fluorescence—will be emitted; and the wavelengths and relative intensities of these secondary X rays will be determined by the elements present. By comparing the secondary emissions from an object of unknown composition with standards based on emissions from known samples, the scientist can tell what elements are present and their approximate concentration. In a matter of minutes equipment can be set up to give an analysis of this type simultaneously covering 14 or more elements.

X-ray fluorescence analysis can indicate only the surface composition of an object, because this is where the secondary X rays come from. Nonetheless, it can often bring to light valuable information. For example, in one laboratory scientists wanting to learn more about the techniques used by craftsmen of the past, as a clue to dating and authenticating Chinese porcelains, sought to distinguish between native and imported cobalt ores used in preparing the blue glaze used in some Chinese pottery. It was known that the native Chinese cobalt ores contained significant amounts of manganese, whereas cobalt ore imported from Persia was quite different; it contained arsenic but no manganese. So by using the technique to determine the relative amounts of cobalt and manganese in the blue glaze in some 80 pieces of porcelain, it was shown that during the 1300s only imported ores were used, that in the 1400s and 1500s both imported and native ores were being used, and after the 1500s only native ores.

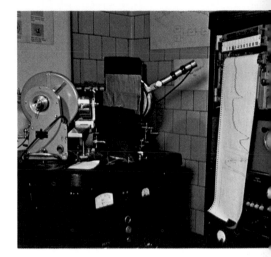

Above: An X-ray diffractometer expresses in graph form the results of an X-ray diffraction analysis on a paint sample.
Below: Francesco di Antonio's *Madonna and Saints* being photographed under a raking light in the Louvre laboratory.
Opposite: The resulting photograph shows the smooth brush strokes used by the artist, and also a crack running down the panel.

The technique of *electron-beam analysis* works on principles similar to that of the X-ray fluorescence analysis. But it is an electron beam, and not an X-ray beam, that is directed onto the target material to make the material produce a burst of X rays. The wavelengths are then analyzed to see what materials are present. With this method it must be realized that only a minute area of a few square microns of surface material is analyzed at any one time (a micron is about a 25,000th part of an inch). Thus the electron-beam technique is ideally suited for carrying out the analysis of very small areas of an object.

The abilities of this set-up were put to a tough test when scientists used it to make an analysis of six different-colored glasses forming a tiny 2,000-year-old Roman mosaic plaque. The plaque itself was only three quarters of an inch square, and some of the individual pieces of glass were less than one sixteenth of an inch across. Nonetheless, the system performed perfectly and gave the scientists the detailed results they were looking for.

X-ray photography also provides the museum laboratory

Left: An "imprisoned" painting. The indistinct figures in this *Holy Family* by Jacob Jordaens were discovered when Jordaens' *Adoration of the Magi* (*below*) was X-rayed in the course of restoration by the Louvre laboratory. Because the paints have fused together, the earlier painting underneath will probably never be seen.

with an important tool for nondestructive examination of antiquities whereby it is possible to show up hidden decoration and inlays, and also to find out the methods used to make the objects. The technique is simple and depends upon the fact that as X rays pass through an object they are absorbed in varying degrees, depending upon the kinds of material incorporated in the object—the greater the density, the greater the absorption. This is exactly the principle that makes X rays useful in medicine. Bone and foreign objects are more dense than muscle, thus they absorb more X rays, while those passing through the flesh react strongly with the film. In museum technique the object to be photographed is placed directly between the source of the X-ray beam and a sheet of film. Since areas that are denser than their surroundings absorb more X rays, inlays, repairs, or additions of metal different from the original will be revealed.

The fact that the pigments used in oil painting vary in their ability to absorb X rays makes X-ray photography a particularly valuable procedure in examining paintings. In 1969 the *Adoration of the Magi*, a painting by Jacob Jordaens, a Flemish artist of the 1600s, was sent by its owners to the Louvre laboratory for cleaning. Using X rays as part of their standard preliminary examination, scientists discovered under the work a clear outline of another painting by Jordaens, this time of the *Holy Family*. The irony of the discovery was that, although experts agreed that the earlier painting was superior to the one on top, there is no way to separate the paintings without destroying both. Oil paint takes anything up to 50 years to dry completely. Fresh paint applied on top before the drying is complete—as in this case—fuses into the lower layer, making separation impossible. It is unlikely that techniques for safe separation will ever be devised. So the world will probably

never see the *Holy Family* by Jordaens except as a ghostly trace on an X-ray plate.

But X rays are only one kind of "invisible" radiation that the museum analyst can put to good use. Infrared and ultraviolet light can also play an important role. Infrared, as its name indicates, is a range of radiation that lies just beyond the red end of the visible spectrum. Simply put, infrared rays are heat rays and can penetrate even dark and illegible areas.

Infrared photography enabled specialists to verify that this painting of the Annunciation —a detail of which is shown here—was truly the work of Juan de Flandes, a Flemish artist who died in 1519.

Infrared light revealed the artist's charcoal under-drawing, whose distinctive shading is typical of the work of this master.

Experts studying and translating old documents often come across some in which passages have been obscured so that they are totally unreadable. But infrared radiation can often come to the rescue. For example, experts deciphering the 2,000-year-old scrolls found near the Dead Sea, were helped enormously by infrared photography. Some of the scrolls were made of leather that had been written upon with ink made of some form of carbon, soot most likely. Over the centuries the leather had blackened and the ink had faded, with the result that the writing could not be made out. But the ancient leather tended to reflect the infrared radiation while the carbon did not. Because of this, the developed infrared photographs showed the leather scrolls as a white background against which the writing stood out clearly.

Similarly, when scientists photographed a painting of the *Annunciation,* believed to be by the Flemish artist Juan de Flandes, under infrared light, it revealed a distinctive shading technique, characteristic of de Flandes' work, in the charcoal under-drawing. Just as in the example of the scrolls, the carbon of the painter's under-drawing did not reflect the infrared while the canvas and ground did. So the drawing with its distinctive shading showed up black against a white background. Experts were able to identify the painting as

de Flandes' work with a certainty otherwise impossible.

Ultraviolet rays can be produced artificially by a mercury vapor lamp. Photography using them can be done in two ways. The first is known as the fluorescent-light method. Normally it is carried out in a darkened room because ultraviolet light will often cause an object to fluoresce, or glow visibly. The glow might appear, for example, on alterations to the surface of the object or painting made at a date later than its origin. A special filter over the lens of the camera will absorb the invisible reflected ultraviolet rays but allow the visible fluorescence to reach the film. The second ultraviolet technique is known as the *reflected-light method*. Here the photograph is made by ultraviolet light reflected from the subject. This time the camera lens is covered by a filter that will let the ultraviolet radiation through but will stop any visible radiation from reaching the film.

There are two further ways in which the camera can help in the laboratory. These are with photomicrography and macrophotography. Photomicrography means taking a photograph through a microscope. With the small 35 mm. cameras it is a simple matter, as an adaptor can be purchased allowing the camera to be fixed to the eyepiece of a microscope. Although the image on the developed 35-mm. film is small, it has recorded every detail the microscope revealed. The obvious advantage is that the image on the film can be further enlarged or projected for easy and leisurely examination.

Macrophotography, almost the opposite of photomicrography, makes use of a bellows extension, extension tubes, or what is known as a "macro lens" on the camera to produce a life-size image of the object on the negative, which then can be enlarged. The advantage over the normal procedure of enlarging a reduced image is that the macro negative, being life-size or nearly so in the first place, will show greater detail and so gives a better quality print when enlarged. It is a method that is very useful when recording small objects such as coins, stamps, and signatures.

The information that scientists in museum laboratories gain as they examine, probe, and analyze objects from the past is of

The use of macrophotography to examine small objects such as coins and stamps is shown in this series of photographs of a British 50 new pence piece. Photograph 1 was taken with a normal lens from a distance of 3 feet—about as close as a normal lens will focus. A life-size image of the coin is obtained by greatly enlarging the print (2), but the result is fuzzy, owing to the grain of the film, which becomes apparent when a photo is enlarged many times. Photograph 3 was taken of the same coin with the same lens, but using extension tubes on the camera. These make it possible to take a sharply focused picture from a distance of only 6 inches, obtaining a life-size image of the coin without enlarging it. Moreover, this original sharp image can be enlarged to get an image that shows tiny details invisible to the naked eye. Photograph 4 shows (3) enlarged almost to the same degree as (2) is to (1). Details of the engraving, chips, and scratches are clearly visible in spite of the film grain, whereas an equally large blow-up of (2) would be only a blur.

vital importance. It enables them not only to authenticate objects and trace them to their original geographical sources, but also to understand in advance what problems they will come up against in restoration work and to act accordingly. The importance of this kind of early warning will be seen more fully in Chapter 5. First, however, a look must be taken at what is probably the most important single area of museum work—the ways in which scientists in today's museums and

3 galleries can put an accurate date on an object or specimen.

4

How Old Is It?

In the early 1600s an Irish priest, Archbishop Usher of Armagh, working from hints he found in the Bible, calculated that God had created the world during the week ending on Saturday, October 22, 4004 B.C. Churchmen were impressed. The English printers of the Authorized Version of the Bible included the Archbishop's date in their edition of 1701, and this gave the date such an air of authoritative certainty that when the geologists of the 1800s suggested that the world was millions of years old, they met with stubborn religious opposition.

Even today, with all the modern dating methods, scientists cannot match the precision of Archbishop Usher. The best they can do is to estimate how old any particular object is, and, the more ancient the object, the shakier the estimate, especially when it comes from one of the very earliest periods, beyond 10 million years or so. As we can see from Usher's exact dating of Creation, precision is not necessarily either accurate or reliable. Although scientific methods can provide only approximate datings, they are considerably more reliable than the Archbishop's calculations and have done much to sort out the difference between objective fact and informed opinion.

Imagine that a Greek terracotta vase has been brought into a museum. Delighted museum officials gather around to admire it. One of the first questions raised is "How old is it?" If the vase turns out to be 2,000 years old it may well have an important place in the museum's display of Greek antiquities. But if it turns out to be a 20-year-old copy, the rubbish heap or the museum cellar is probably the best place for it.

There are two quite different ways of answering this important question. One way is to call in a man who has dealt with ancient Greek vases all his life. He will examine the style of the vase and its method of manufacture. By applying a certain intuitive touch born of knowledge and experience, he will probably be able either to say it is 2,000 years old and, in his opinion, genuine, or to dismiss it as a fake. There have, however, been many experts who have dated and identified an object by experience and intuition but have later found that they have acclaimed as a masterpiece a worthless fake, or,

A deep-sea diver salvages a barnacle-encrusted Greek wine jar from the ocean floor, where it has lain for 2,000 years.
Opposite: This Greek terracotta vase, depicting Theseus killing the Minotaur, dates from the sixth century B.C. Knowledge of art styles and periods helps the museum curator assign a date to an object such as this one, but laboratory tests can confirm or disprove his estimate.

more rarely, rejected as fake an item of great worth. More often than not, as a back-up at least, museum officials will turn the vase over to a laboratory scientist, who will apply a number of special tests and come up with a table of facts. The advantage of a series of complex physical and chemical tests is that they provide a set of reliable observations on which to base a dating. True, the facts still need interpretation, but they do have the advantage of being free of human judgment and subjective opinion.

In the late 1940s an American physicist, Willard F. Libby of the University of Chicago, developed a new way of dating archaeological specimens that contained carbon. His method, called *radiocarbon dating,* is based on the fact that in all samples of carbon there are a few atoms (one in about a million million) of what is called *heavy carbon.* In every way, atoms of heavy carbon are chemically identical to ordinary carbon atoms. The difference is solely a matter of atomic weight. The most common form of carbon has an atomic weight of 12, whereas that of heavy carbon is 14. Heavy carbon is also radioactive. That is, its atoms emit radiation and in so doing gradually break down by a process known as radioactive decay to form a non-radioactive nitrogen.

Libby worked on the theory that there is a relatively constant supply of heavy carbon mixed in with the carbon in the air and the tissues of living organisms. While they are alive, animals and plants maintain the constant proportion of heavy carbon in their tissues—they remain in equilibrium with the global carbon exchange reservoir. When plants and animals die, however, the intake of carbon of any kind ceases, and the atoms of heavy carbon already in their tissues continue to break down into nitrogen, with the result that the radioactivity of the dead organism's tissues falls off in a regular manner. According to the *law of radioactive decay* the rate at which any radioactive substance breaks down to a non-radioactive atom is measured by its half-life. In the case of heavy carbon this is 5,600 years, which means that if originally there were, say, 1,000 atoms of heavy carbon in a substance, 5,600 years later there will be, on the average, only 500 atoms left—the rest will have decayed. In another 5,600 years only 250 radioactive carbon atoms will be left, and the process continues until all the heavy carbon has decayed. At each stage, then, the total amount of radioactivity of the substance decreases by half.

Libby saw that by using a special detecting device rather like a supersensitive geiger counter, he could measure the radioactivity of the heavy carbon in, say, a sliver of wood taken from an ancient dugout canoe. If he then compared it with that of a piece of living wood and with anthracite (which was originally living wood, but is so old that for all practical

Equipment for radiocarbon dating. The object to be tested is placed in the cabinet, which contains a Geiger counter, used to measure the radioactivity of materials.

purposes it has lost all radioactivity), he could use the law of radioactive decay to calculate how long ago it was since the canoe was carved from a newly cut tree.

The first experimental checks on the accuracy of radiocarbon dating were made on samples of an already known date. The method was tried out on wood from the graves of Egyptian pharaohs, which had been dated on chronological grounds through historical research. Excitement ran high when the dates given by Libby's technique came to within 10 per cent of the already established dates.

Radiocarbon dating has already changed many previously held ideas about geological and archaeological happenings. For example, prior to Libby's work geologists had always thought that the last advance of the Wisconsin glaciation passed over North America 25,000 years ago, but radiocarbon dating of ancient tree trunks buried in the glacial morains has shown it was only 11,400 years ago. Small pieces from rope sandals covered by volcanic deposits in Oregon were dated to about 7000 B.C. These sandals are the oldest known man-made objects yet found in the Western Hemisphere, and may possibly date from near the time when man first appeared in the Americas.

The results of radiocarbon dating are never completely precise. They are usually given within a range of possible error stated as plus or minus 300 years. The actual date could lie anywhere between. Using radiocarbon dating equipment, laboratory examination was made of a piece of deer antler found near one of the great stones at Stonehenge in England. It was estimated that it was 3,670 years old (plus or minus 300 years). But as we try to date older and older specimens the margin of the possible error grows. In practice, radiocarbon dating gives useful results going back about 40,000 years. Beyond that point the possible error becomes so large that the result is not usually of much value.

Archaeological evidence suggested that these antlers found at Stonehenge, in southern England, were about 3,600 years old. Radiocarbon dating gave a figure of 3,670, plus or minus 150 years.

Late in 1663 the great British scientist Robert Boyle was shown a remarkable jewel by a friend. As Boyle excitedly reported to the Royal Society in London shortly afterwards, the gem " . . . being rubbed upon my clothes . . . did in the dark manifestly shine like rotten wood, or the scales of whiting or other putrified fish . . . much fainter than the light of a glow-worm." Boyle had not witnessed a piece of wizardry. The glow he had seen was what is known as *thermoluminescence*. The phenomenon is widely used today by archaeologists all over the world as a basis for dating specimens, especially fragments of ancient pottery.

This is how it works. Most mineral substances contain traces of radioactive material—uranium or thorium salts for instance. But some minerals are able to store in their crystalline lattice the energy produced by this radioactivity, and when heated release it in the form of visible light. This was the glow that Boyle had seen after he had heated the object by rubbing it on his coat. Most thermoluminescent substances, however, need to be heated to over 640°F before they will glow. Even then the light given off is often almost too feeble for the naked eye to see, but there are sensitive detecting devices available to measure the light's intensity. Roughly speaking, the brighter the glow, the older the mineral. So by measuring the stored energy in this way, scientists can work out how long the mineral had been absorbing the energy from the radioactive traces it contains.

When it comes to dating pottery, this technique has particular importance, for most of the clay minerals used in making pottery can store thermoluminescence. During the original firing of the clay to make pottery all the energy previously stored by the clay minerals is wiped out, because the intense heat releases any stored energy. After firing, however, the clay starts to build up its store of energy again. So any thermoluminescence that a scientist finds will be due to energy accumulated after this point. Any estimate he arrives at by measuring the stored energy will date the object to the moment when it was fired.

An exhibition organized in 1970 in London highlighted the value of the technique. Hundreds of ceramic figures from the Sui and T'ang dynasties of China (A.D. 589-907) were put on display. All the items had their dates proved by thermo-luminescent testing. For the first time organizers of a display of this kind could be confident that the items really were what their owners claimed them to be.

Atoms of some minerals keep the secret of their age in a number of other ways. For instance, almost all clays contain at least a small amount of iron oxides. Each minute particle of iron oxide behaves like a tiny magnet. A lump of

Growth rings can be clearly seen on this cross section of a tree trunk. There is one growth ring for each year, indicating that the tree was about 45 years old when it was chopped down.

clay freshly dug from the earth has no apparent remanent magnetism, however, because all the tiny magnets inside it are arranged haphazardly, and in the jumble they cancel each other out. But if a lump of clay is heated above 1,270°F and then allowed to cool, the miniature magnets align themselves along any predominant magnetic field that happens to be around. Usually this turns out to be the earth's magnetic field—that is, they line themselves up along the earth's magnetic north-south axis. In other words the clay has become a weak permanent magnet with a definite direction of magnetization.

What makes this process valuable as a means of dating is that a true magnetic bearing of any point on earth varies with time. For example, in London the angle between the line joining the North and South geographic poles (which never changes) and the magnetic north-south axis has varied by about 10 degrees over each century during the last 500 years. Similar changes have been found and recorded in other parts of the world.

Once we know the direction of the earth's magnetic axis as it was at the time of firing, the date of firing can be easily established. We need only consult the records for the appropriate world region to see how the direction has altered over the past few centuries. Then, working backward, we can find

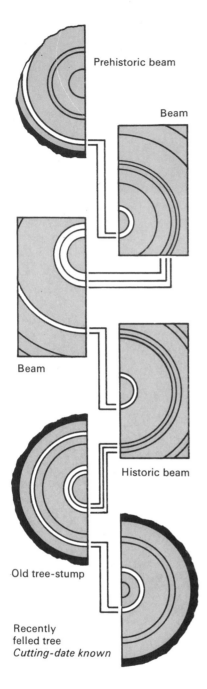

Prehistoric beam

Beam

Beam

Historic beam

Old tree-stump

Recently
felled tree
Cutting-date known

when the direction had the particular value recorded in the clay. So by measuring the direction of magnetization of a piece of fired clay, we are, in fact, measuring the direction of the earth's magnetic north-south axis as it was when the clay was last fired. But a limitation on this method of dating is immediately obvious. The fired clay must not have been moved at all since its last firing. If it has been moved its magnetization will tell us nothing about its relationship to the past direction of the earth's magnetic axis. In practice, then, we can only use this approach in dating ancient clay ovens and kilns, the kind of clay objects that are rarely moved even over the centuries.

Almost any natural phenomenon that will give a time series, which is all that a calendar is, really, can be put to use in archaeological dating. For some purposes and in some regions tree rings have proved most helpful.

The basic principles of tree-ring dating can be studied by anyone who visits a site where trees are being cut down. A quick examination of a fallen trunk shows a succession of light and dark rings; each light ring represents one year's growth and is known as an annual ring. The difference in thickness between these annual rings can be produced by variations in climate. A dry summer results in a narrow ring. A wet summer in a thick ring. Further, the rings tend to become narrower as a tree grows older.

The significance of the annual growth tree-rings has been realized for a long time. The first archaeological application was made, however, in 1811. The American De Witt Clinton counted the rings of some trees that had grown over earthworks near Canandaigua in New York State and found the trees had been growing for several hundred years. This gave him enough information to conclude that the constructions were not the work of the Indians of his time or of early European settlers, but must have been made by some prehistoric peoples.

Between 1901 and 1913 another American, Dr. A. E. Douglass, director of the Arizona University Observatory, was involved in studying minor solar variations, and relating them to climatic conditions in the Southwest. He found that official meteorological records for the area went back less than 100 years. Thus he had no clear pattern of climatic fluctuations to extend his theory of solar variation back into past time. But knowing the effect of varying climates on tree rings, he turned to a study of woods like the pitron pine and the yellow western pine that have clear growth rings. From his researches relating tree rings to postclimates he evolved an approach to dating that could be used to date ancient buildings if timbers had been used in their construction (see diagram and caption on this page). He produced evidence to show that some inhabited sites of the Pueblo Indians in Arizona went back 1,900 years.

In Europe tree-ring dating is more difficult than in the south-western United States, because of climatic conditions, which show considerable variations of temperature and humidity between years. Nevertheless, by investigating a number of different types of trees and working with known felling dates a method of plotting of annual ring widths on logarithmic ordinates has been developed to establish an accurate tree-ring chronology. Using data from the annual rings of larch trees in the Bavarian Alps around Berchtesgaden, one scientist has worked out an accurate tree-ring dating that goes back satisfactorily to A.D. 1300.

Some experts in this field of research have investigated the variations in the sequence of thick and thin rings in European trees and also with similar trees in America. It has been thought that there could be a relationship between these sequences, a so-called "teleconnection," but at the moment no really reliable information can be proved. One fascinating fact does emerge, however, and that is, an 11-year cycle of ring thicknesses may be related to the 11-year sun-spot cycles.

One of the most interesting developments from tree-ring dating is that it has given a useful clue to an American expedition searching in the region of Mount Arrarat in Turkey for the remains of the Ark. They have been given hope by the fact that a few years ago a French archaeologist discovered in a crevice some 14,000 feet up the mountain some pieces of hewn oak estimated to be about 5,000 years old. Since oak trees do not grow naturally on Mount Arrarat, this find lent some strength to American expectations that they might eventually locate the Ark, perhaps at the bottom of some deep lake nearby.

This illustration from a medieval manuscript shows Noah and his Ark. Its wooden construction has been rendered in some detail.

The Restorers

The treasures that fill our museums and galleries are not always as safe as we imagine. Despite every effort to keep them well guarded, collections often come under attack from unsuspected sources. Besides light, moisture (or lack of it), and polluted air, the enemies of the treasure keepers include bacteria, molds, insects, and man.

If the air is too warm and damp, bacteria and molds are encouraged to grow. And if their growth is unchecked they will cause rot in canvas and wood and discolor and stain the

This detail from the *Rokeby Venus* by Velázquez. A demonstrator for women's rights entered London's National Gallery one morning in 1914 and made seven slashes in the painting (*right*). The picture was retouched at the time, but subsequent cleaning and retouching has restored the painting to its earlier brilliance.

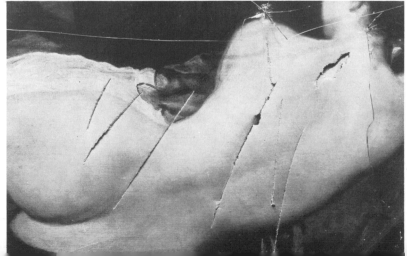

A picture that tells some of the sad story of the flood damage in Florence. Racks hold the wrecked books while they dry out, so that they can then be tackled by the restorers. Each book will have to be dismembered, and the separate pages cleaned and laboriously resewn together and rebound.

surfaces of paintings, books, and other precious treasures. Damp heat in particular is a menace in libraries where it will favor the growth of molds on the leather bindings of books. But if the air is too dry, painted surfaces and the paper and leather of books and manuscripts become dangerously brittle. While the physical environment goes about its job of destruction with slow but grim efficiency, the attack by living agents may be more direct. Beetles and termites, for instance, burrow into wood, sometimes fatally weakening a whole carving.

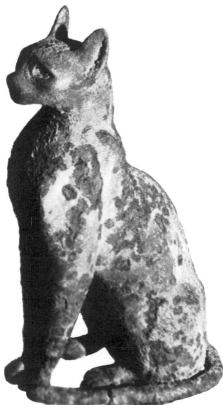

The human attack may be even more vicious. Vandals cannot resist leaving behind reminders of their visits—often their initials, but sometimes more. In 1914 Mary Richardson, a demonstrator for women's rights, visited London's National Gallery and used a hatchet on the beautiful *Rokeby Venus* by the Spanish painter Velázquez. In 1962 a maniac damaged 25 paintings worth almost $2,000,000 in the Uffizi Gallery, Florence. At the Louvre, Paris, *La Source* by the French painter Ingres has had to be covered with glass to stop visitors from scribbling all over it.

The men and women who fight the decay, repair damage, and protect against further troubles are the restorers. Their work falls into two categories. The first is the cleaning of

48

The desire of vandals to leave their mark behind is nothing new. This 400-year-old alabaster carving of a baby in Gloucester Cathedral, England, provides mute evidence of the senseless damage to works of art caused by thoughtless or deranged individuals.

Severe "bronze disease" on an early Egyptian cast of a cat. Certain salts are present in the layers of early bronzes. If such objects are exposed to excessive moisture, this will activate the salts and produce surface evidence with the appearance of light green spots.

newly found treasures and then strengthening those that are fragile—a process known as *consolidation*. The second is maintaining and preserving those already in galleries and museums. Most restorers specialize in one of the many fields, such as metals, textiles, ceramics, glass, or paintings, a few may work in several. Sometimes the restorer can do little more than despair over a terribly mutilated work of art—a rotten and discolored canvas, or an insect-riddled wooden statue. More often than not, however, he can use the growing armory of scientific aids to work near-miracles of restoration.

Gold is unique among metals in that it is almost indestructible. It does not tarnish or corrode. Thus, nearly a century ago, when the German archaeologist Heinrich Schliemann discovered the 3,000-year-old "Mask of Agamemnon" at Mycenae, it appeared almost exactly as it had been when buried. But preserving and restoring metals other than gold can often produce great headaches for the restorer. He may have to deal with silver, copper, iron, tin, an alloy such as bronze, pewter, and steel, or combinations of these. Some may rust, others tarnish, and yet others are prone to a so-called "disease"—really a form of chemical corrosion—such as that which attacks bronze and causes it to crumble. Sometimes, too, a metal may react with chemical substances in the soil or air to form new mineral compounds to such an extent that the original metallic material is completely lost. Such was the case of the famous Silver Lyre from Ur, now on display in the British Museum.

In 1927 a team of archaeologists led by Sir Leonard Woolley excavated a series of 4,000-year-old royal tombs near the site of the ancient city of Ur of the Chaldees, in what is now Iraq. Woolley spent 12 years at Ur in the twenties and thirties excavating on behalf of the British Museum and the University Museum of Pennsylvania. When he opened the Great Death Pit, a burial site dating from about 2500 B.C., he found not only the skeletons of courtiers and servants, slain to serve their king and queen in the after-life, but also less grisly relics—a collection of jewelry and musical instruments, including the remains of nine lyres—harp-like instruments stopped with the left hand and plucked with a plectrum held in the right.

Above: The Silver Lyre of Ur as it was discovered, crushed and broken, in the "Great Death Pit" in 1927, having lain buried for some 4,000 years.

Below: This detail from the Standard of Ur, a mosaic depicting the life of a Sumerian king, shows a musician playing a lyre similar to the one discovered in the "Great Death Pit."

One of the lyres, all of which were crushed and broken when discovered, was skillfully reassembled on a new wooden framework. The reconstruction was helped by reference to the Royal Standard of Ur, which bears a representation of a lyre. After reconstruction this instrument, once resplendent with silver decoration, was shown for many years in the Department of Western Asiatic Antiquities in the British Museum. It did not, however, look like a silver lyre because it was, quite simply, a silver chloride lyre. During its nearly 4,000-year burial, corrosion had almost completely converted the metallic silver into silver chloride. Microscopic examination of a fragment showed that only tiny particles of silver had escaped mineralization, as this kind of chemical reaction is called.

Left: The lyre as it appeared when it was reconstructed on a wooden framework. Some of the decoration has been restored, but mineralization had converted virtually all of the original silver into silver chloride.

Generally, when ancient objects of silver have only a thin mineralized surface, the plan of action is to reverse the process and change the silver chloride by chemical means back into powdery metallic silver that can be brushed off to show the underlying silver. In the case of the Chaldean lyre, however, there was practically no solid silver remaining, so an entirely new technique of electrolytic reduction—as the change from silver chloride to silver is called—had to be worked out.

After trials with small fragments of the lyre, a special procedure of what may be called consolidative reduction to give massive coherent silver was adopted. The main pieces of the lyre were backed with a film of plastic embedded with silver wires to conduct the electric current. This set-up would become the negative electrode. Then the plastic-backed pieces of the lyre were lowered into a tank containing a five per cent solution of caustic soda to which a carbon rod was added as the positive electrode. When a very light current was passed through the solution, the dark silver chloride slowly began to break down to yield massive coherent silver, which could be polished to shine with a bright metallic sheen.

Swords, armor, guns, and other destructive tools of man's warlike past are part of history's treasure. The fact that they are very largely made from iron or steel means that in anything approaching a damp climate they rust and pit very easily, and this puts them among the most difficult objects for the restorer to treat. With any heavily corroded or rusted iron or steel object the first task in the museum laboratory is to examine it thoroughly. It may be that, as in the case of the mineralized Chaldean lyre, the metal has all but disappeared. Because the ugly layers of rust may conceal inlay or other delicate decorations, the restorer will make sure that X-ray photographs are taken to reveal any patterns of decoration beneath the rust. Next comes the problem of determining whether the object is too delicate to withstand more than a bare minimum of treatment or whether, below the surface, there is still a fairly

Left: After being subjected to a process called electrolytic reduction, the lyre is literally transformed back to nearly its original appearance.

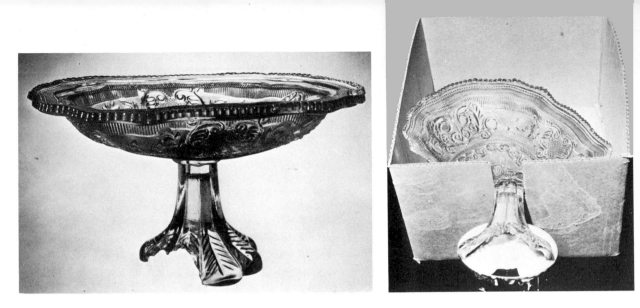

strong core of metal left. Examination of the surface with a binocular microscope, and probing with a fine needle, give an idea of the depth of the corrosion.

When the extent of the problem is known, the restorer can decide how to deal with it. If the object is indeed very delicate, it may be necessary to confine restoration to removing as much rust as can be done safely by hand, using fine scrapers for the purpose. If, on the other hand, it still has a fairly strong core of metal, the procedure of choice will probably be what is called *electrochemical reduction*. This chemical reaction is the opposite of rusting, and converts iron oxide, which is the chemical name of rust, to metal. To do this with small objects of iron, technicians bury them in zinc in a suitable container, which is then filled with a solution of sodium hydroxide. The liquid is boiled and distilled water is added as necessary to keep the object covered with solution. When the piece cools, much of the deposit of corrosion can be gently brushed away under running water.

Below: One of the two scrolls from Qumran, a rigid roll of corroded copper.
Below, left: Having been coated with plastic to prevent it from crumbling, the scroll is mounted on the spindle and cut with a very thin circular saw into narrow strips, which can then be assembled and deciphered.

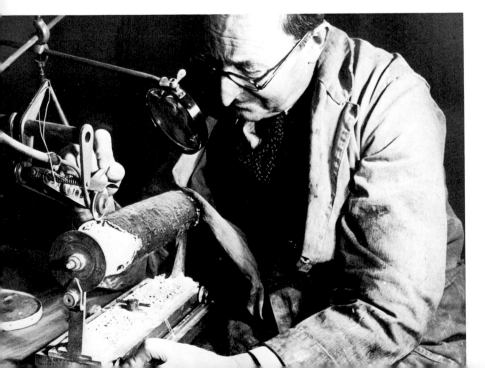

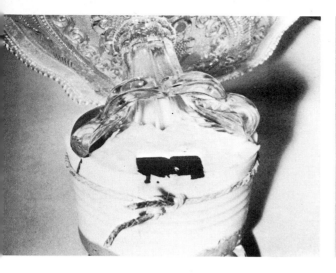

The restoration of glassware often poses some of the most difficult problems for the conservator. The material by its very nature does not lend itself to completely successful treatment; nearly always the joins will remain visible. Whichever technique is used, the object must be adequately supported. When a mold is made, this is generally from latex, and great care is called for during the whole process. A slight error could be very difficult to correct, as the method may not always be reversible.

One of the greatest challenges that experts in corroded metals have ever faced began when an intriguing archaeological find was made in Qumran, near the Dead Sea in the Israeli-occupied territory of Jordan. For several years archaeologists throughout the world had been in a ferment of excitement following the discovery of the Dead Sea Scrolls (see pages 67-68). But those scrolls were of leather or parchment. On March 14, 1952, something new came to light. In the exploration of a cave whose roof had long since fallen in, choking it with rock, two scrolls of a very different kind were brought to light. Originally they had been rolls of pliable sheet copper, about 11 inches wide, but over the years, chemical reaction with the atmosphere had changed them into brittle copper oxide. The scholars were tantalized by the indentations of ancient Aramaic or Hebrew letters they could see from the outside, and were desperately anxious to read these ancient writings. It was clear, however, that any attempt at unrolling would crumble the brittle copper oxide, and leave the scholars with nothing but a pile of metallic dust.

Fortunately, wisdom prevailed. The scrolls were coated with paraffin wax to preserve them, and taken to the Palestine Archaeological Museum. There they lay for three years while scientists tried to work out a way of unrolling them. Methods of reconstituting corroded metals that had proved useful in other archaeological fields were of no avail. The corrosion had gone so far there seemed to be no chance of restoring the strength and pliability required to unroll the weakened copper.

Finally it was decided that the only hope of ever reading the scrolls was to coat the outside with a plastic that would hold the frail material together, and cut them into strips. The task was undertaken by technicians at the College of Technology in Manchester, England. They mounted the plastic-coated rolls one at a time on the spindle of a specially prepared cutting machine. The essential working part of the machine was an extremely thin circular saw two inches in diameter. It could be delicately adjusted to a depth of cut precisely of the thickness of the copper sheet.

As the saw first bit into the ancient scroll moving slowly along on a trolley beneath the saw, scientists and technicians held their breath. The first narrow strip came free without breaking, and from then on it was clear that the technique would work. To cut the entire eight-foot length of the two scrolls into strips, clean each strip, and assemble the whole into correct sequence was a slow and laborious job. At last, four years after the rolls had been recovered from the cave, scholars were able to decipher their message. The effort was a technical triumph. For scholars, however, the results were disappointing. Unlike the Dead Sea Scrolls discovered before them, the copper scrolls shed no new light on the Scriptures. Instead they gave details of a hoard of treasure that had probably been hidden from the Romans more than 2,000 years ago.

Early man made many of the things that he used from bone. Hunters tipped their arrows with bone and fishermen made their hooks from it. Ancient artists and priests scratched pictures on shoulder blades and other flat pieces of bone. Ivory, too, was also used for objects both useful and decorative. Many an important clue to man's past has been found on bits of bone and ivory worked by unknown craftsmen of antiquity. Both bone and ivory, however, are likely to be damaged by moisture and heat. Dampness may start decomposition, while a dry, hot atmosphere may cause splitting and cracking. Since both of these materials are moderately porous, they can easily be stained by substances with which they have come in contact. Bright sunshine will bleach them. Time makes them fragile.

The puzzle for the restorer, when confronted with a newly dug up artifact of bone or ivory, is how to clean it. It is likely to be covered with clay, salts, or other incrustations and may also be very delicate. The archaeologist who originally found the piece will have dug it out together with a good deal of surrounding earth to protect it. When the artifact reaches the museum laboratory the restorer must first gently pry away

A silver cup from Enkomi, Cyprus (15th century B.C.), shown left, as it was found and as it appeared on arrival at the Research Laboratory at the British Museum. The silver, inlaid with gold and niello, is completely covered with corrosion products. X-ray examination showed the original decoration. The cup was treated with formic acid, which successfully removed the incrustation. Final patches of cuprite and reduced copper yielded to local applications of ammonia. At right, the restored cup.

A very delicate operation is the separation of two icons, one painted on top of the other. The icon (right) was painted around the end of the 18th century on top of another icon (above) painted some 200 years earlier. Because icons are regarded as holy objects in the Eastern Orthodox faith, they must not be destroyed. When they became darkened, through the effect of candle smoke on the oil that was rubbed on the surface to make them shine, they were often repainted with a new image. The presence of the original icon was detected by X ray (left). A new and delicate process allows the two icons to be separated.

the clinging earth with the help of a soft wooden probe, and he may find the object—let's say a finely carved ivory statuette of an Egyptian household god—to be very brittle. How is this frail object to be further cleaned?

The answer is that it can be washed—but only in a rather special manner. The whole process must be done in as short a time as possible to prevent further damage to the specimen caused by any prolonged soaking in water. The first step is to immerse the carving in a bath of distilled water for a few seconds only. The restorer then removes it from the bath, changes the water, and repeats the whole process four or five times. Next the carving is washed in alcohol to remove the water, and then in ether (which speeds up evaporation) before it is left to dry thoroughly in air.

If the restorer feels the ancient ivory piece is too fragile to be washed just as it is, it may first have to be given some form of protection. This can be done by brushing on a coat of soluble nylon, which dries to cover the specimen with a very remarkable tough protective film that supports the object. The washing water however, can pass freely through it, reach the surface of the ivory, dissolve away any adhering salts, and pass freely back again.

After the incrusting salts and dirt are cleaned off, the little god may still be very delicate. The restorer will then impregnate it with a plastic resin to consolidate it. The real problem is to make sure that all the tiny pores and cavities in the ivory carving (which are the cause of its weakness) are filled with the resin. If the restorer finds that just brushing the resin on won't do the job satisfactorily or that the decorative carving is too fragile to take the quite firm brush strokes needed, what can be done? The answer is to immerse the god in a container filled with the resin and place it in a vacuum chamber. When the air is pumped out of the chamber the pressure drops inside the container. Air trapped in the tiny cavities of the ivory is sucked out, and resin replaces it. When no more air bubbles escape from the ivory the restorer releases the vacuum, removes the object, and leaves it to drain until it is dry.

Finally, the cleaned and consolidated statuette can be examined and classified. It is now ready for the museum showcase. But few museum visitors will realize the problems that had to be overcome before it could find its way into the museum's display.

One material that is usually troublesome is leather, particularly if it is very old. We know that Paleolithic man used animal skins, but we do not know exactly when people began to preserve skins by curing and making the hides into leather. It may be that the earliest curing method was to soften the hardened skins with brains and fat, in a manner similar to that later used to make soft leathers such as chamois. Excavations on Paleolithic sites have produced primitive skin-scrapers of flint and bone, which could have been used to remove the hair and remnants of flesh or fat from the inside of the skin. It is interesting to note that a number of these very early implements seem to have been used throughout the ages with little change in design, and have even left their influence on the tools we use for similar purposes today.

Rawhide, when still wet and glutinous, can be molded into a shape it will retain on drying. Graves at Mostagedda in Egypt dating from about 4000 B.C. have produced clay forms that could have been used for shaping rawhide pots. Since that time all manner of articles have been made from molded leather. There have been satchels for religious relics and manuscripts, water buckets, containers for wine and ale, spectacle cases, and snuff boxes. The ability of leather to retain a molded shape when it dries is still exploited in decorative book bindings, decorated baggage, and harness.

During its history, leather has been tanned or cured in many different ways, and the method of tanning or curing very often affects restoration techniques. Probably one of the earliest methods of curing a hide was by smoking it, as is still done sometimes by Eskimos. Until quite recent years it was not uncommon for old Eskimo women to have teeth worn down to the gums, because they often chewed the skin to soften it before it was cured.

A number of substances such as salt, oil, alum, and tannin used in leather-making raise special problems for the restorer. Alum was used to produce a white, stiff material called tawed leather, which was widely used by the ancient sea-going peoples of the Mediterranean. Caesar tells of sails for ships made from tawed leather. It is uncertain when tannin was first used as a preservative for leather, but we do know it was used by ancient Egyptians. Their only available source of tannin appears to have been oak galls, the round swellings on oak trees caused by an insect depositing its eggs.

Just how complicated leather-making processes sometimes were is shown by this recipe from ancient Babylonia: "The skin of the kid thou shalt feed with milk of a yellow goat and with flour; thou shalt anoint it with pure oil . . . . Thou shalt dilute alum in pressed grape-juice, then fill the surface with gall-nuts [presumably in a liquid state] of the tree cultivators of the Hittites."

When materials that have been treated in such complicated ways suffer the effects of air pollution, excessive

Marble is notoriously difficult to clean, as casual applications can drive stains farther into the material. Latest techniques favor the use of a poultice of sepiolite mixed with a cleaning agent. This is applied to the object and allowed to dry. The action of evaporation draws the stains out of the marble and into the poultice, which when dry can be brushed away.

dryness or dampness, and attacks by insects, quite a problem can arise. It is no wonder that museums do their best to keep such damaging effects at bay.

Yet, even when all reasonable precautions seem to have been taken, unexpected dangers can arise. The British Museum found this out the hard way. A few years ago there was a minor flood in one of the museum's basement rooms where books were stored. After draining the water and checking that no books had been damaged, the relative humidity was measured. The flood had driven the relative humidity above the danger level, but the situation was quickly corrected by the use of fans and heaters.

The books were thought to be safe. One important factor had been overlooked, however. Although the *average* relative humidity of the room was perfect, pockets of stagnant air had formed here and there, and in these localized pockets a relative humidity far above the danger level still persisted. During a routine check some while after the flood, a museum technician removed a book from the metal shelving. To his horror he found mold growing on its leather binding. The whole process of drying out had to be repeated once again, and each book checked and treated.

In tropical countries where humidity and temperature are high, museums cannot always afford the air-conditioning equipment needed to control their environments. In small rural museums there is simply not enough cash available to keep dehumidifiers running all year round.

The large numbers of insects in tropical and near-tropical and temperate climates present another problem. The way to avoid any real danger from insects is quite simple: good housekeeping. Insects are attracted by dirt, so regular cleaning of exhibits and their cases goes far toward keeping them at bay. A careful check during cleaning will show up any sign of insects before they have time to spread. If the signs are spotted early enough, the exhibit can at once be removed from its case and sprayed with an insecticide. Although the treatment must be powerful enough to wipe out every insect, it must not harm the leather or other materials of which the objects are made. Nowadays museums can choose from a number of insecticides that have been developed specifically for these purposes.

Yet occasionally—perhaps because of someone's inattention or because a specimen has been infested when brought in—a really serious outbreak of insect attack will occur. Drastic problems call for drastic measures, and a very powerful killer is then needed for effective treatment. Both hydrogen cyanide and carbon disulfide are good answers to the problem, but both must be used with tremendous care. One lungful of hydrogen cyanide will kill a man instantly. Carbon disulfide can explode if there is flame nearby. So specimens to be treated with either one must first be placed in a fume cabinet.

Too little moisture in the air is as bad for leather as too much. Long exposure to a dry atmosphere turns leather and hides of all types hard and brittle. For example, archaeologists have often discovered remarkably well-preserved human bodies in ancient desert tombs in the Middle East. But although skin still clings to the bones, even after thousands of years, it is invariably as dry and brittle as frail parchment. When exposed to the air it will crumble to dust at a touch. Thin sheets of leather can be affected in just the same way.

If the brittle condition is noticed soon enough, and if the leather has not been shaped under tension in such a way that shrinkage will harm it, the restorer's task is not difficult. In mild cases he simply applies a cream made from lanolin and wax. The wax is absorbed and lubricates the inner fibers, thus restoring their elasticity. The lanolin remains on the brittle outer surface of the leather and consolidates it. However, in bookbindings and other molded leather objects, the leather was originally tensioned by shrinkage as it dried. In such a case an application of a cream of lanolin and wax

Left: The 17th-century Swedish warship *Vasa* being sprayed with water and special waxes, called polyethylene glycols, to strengthen the weakened cells of the wood—submerged for more than 300 years.

Far left: This skeleton, still wearing shoes, was found in the *Vasa,* which sank on her maiden voyage during a squall. *Left*: The *Vasa* in dry dock after being salvaged from the bottom of Stockholm Harbor.

Before its treatment with epoxy resin, this ceremonial Nigerian mask had deteriorated to a fragile shell —the wood eaten away by insects. The resin, mixed with a hardener, was applied to the mask in a liquid state. Rock hard when set, the resin reinforced the mask so that it could be displayed.

without preliminary treatment would restore elasticity and might shrink the leather still more, very likely damaging it in the process. In cases of this kind the leather must first be relaxed by prolonged soaking in distilled water. Only after it is relaxed can the cream safely be applied.

Leather objects that have lain in the desert for centuries may become as hard as rock. What the restorer then does is to saturate the leather with a man-made lubricating wax. He immerses the leather in a vat of molten wax and leaves it to soak for several days. The process can work wonders, reviving the natural flexibility of fibers that have taken on an almost stone-like hardness during centuries of drying.

Probably about the same time that early man learned the art of making stone tools to work leather, he also turned them to working wood. Many of the treasures in modern museums are wooden, and most are subject to deterioration from atmospheric effects, as well as to attacks of insects. One of the most spectacular restorations of wood was the work needed to reclaim the Swedish ship *Vasa*. In August, 1628, this proud warship set sail on her maiden voyage from the quay of the Royal Palace in Stockholm. Suddenly disaster struck. Only a hundred yards or so off shore in Stockholm Harbor the *Vasa* was hit by a squall, capsized, and sank in only 110 feet of water.

Just over 300 years were to pass before the great bulk, submerged and nearly forgotten, was rediscovered almost by accident. In April, 1961, a salvage team working for the Swedish government succeeded in raising the magnificent example of 17th-century shipbuilding. Wood that has lain in water or moist ground for many years has been weakened— sometimes disastrously so—because the cellulose of its cell walls has rotted. The real damage is done when wood in this condition begins to dry out. If the water held inside the cells evaporates, the weakened cell walls collapse inward, causing the wood to shrink and disintegrate.

A vast amount of work was necessary to prevent the *Vasa* from falling to pieces from the effects of drying. She was put immediately into a gigantic shower bath, where powerful sprays working day and night poured more than 500 gallons of water a minute over every inch of her hull and super-structure. While this went on, a housing was built over the ship. Once the protective shelter was complete, the air inside

Two clay tablets before and after cleaning. After several thousand years, the cuneiform inscriptions had become illegible, due to the gradual accumulation of salts on the tablets. The fragile, unbaked tablets were fired in a kiln, making them durable and making it possible to remove the incrusted salts without damaging the objects themselves.

was kept almost saturated with moisture. Sprays continued to play over the timbers, but now the water contained additives according to formulas worked out by teams of experts. These included special waxes to strengthen the wood fibers, and various chemicals to stop any rotting. Periodically a fungicide was added to destroy any algae or fungi that might be getting hold of the wood fibers.

The waxes used in the *Vasa* operation are of a type known as polyethylene glycols. They provide the most effective treatment of waterlogged wood although their most frequent successes have been with objects much smaller than warships. Unlike all other waxes, the polyethylene glycols are soluble in water. This remarkable property permits the tricky process of removing water from damaged wood cells and replacing it with consolidating wax to be carried out in one step. The restorer puts the wooden object into a container filled with a water and wax mixture. The tightly covered container is placed in a ventilated oven where the temperature is built up to about 140°F, and held there over a period of weeks. During that time the wax slowly seeps into the wood, gently forcing out the water from the delicate cells. The water, in turn, evaporates and escapes through a hole in the container. Eventually the wood becomes completely saturated and covered with wax. When the object has cooled, the restorer carefully removes the wax coating from its outer surface. Below the surface the once fragile wood cells are now bolstered with a filling of hardened wax, and much of the object's original strength has been restored.

Wood heavily damaged by insects demands a similar strengthening technique. Certain insects, particularly the larvae of beetles, can riddle a wooden object with holes and reduce it to a fragile husk in a very short time.

This was the condition of an African ceremonial mask brought to British Museum experts for restoration some years ago.

The strange double-faced, four-horned mask had been carved in Nigeria by an old Ibo craftsman about 1900. And now, half a century later, the dark wood still seemed to ring with the music and chanting of the rituals for which the mask had been made. But insects had reduced it to a mere shell, weak and hollow. The slightest mishandling would crush it. The nose of one face and one ear were about ready to fall off.

The British Museum impregnated the wood with a plastic material that would set rock hard. The plastic they chose was a type known as epoxy resin. What was new about this

technique was that the resin, mixed with a special hardener, was applied in a fluid state, and then hardened inside the wood. Previously, molten waxes would have been applied. But was, when set, could never match the rock-hard support of a resin filling. The method worked well to restore much of the strength of the mask so that the work of the Ibo craftsman could safely be shown to the public.

Paint complicates the job of consolidating wooden objects. The paint itself must be protected lest waxes or chemicals damage it or dull the original colors. What restorers usually do is cover or face the painted surface with a protective layer of tissue paper, applied with an adhesive that insures the

Modern techniques of cleaning can achieve dramatic results —as in the case of Titian's *Bacchus and Ariadne,* one of the treasures of London's National Gallery. The painstaking task of removing the layers of old varnish took restorers nearly two years.

facing can be removed easily without damage to the paint. Once the job of consolidating the wood as a whole has been done, the tissue paper is removed.

This is simple enough. Often, however, the paint layer itself is in a bad state, sometimes on the verge of falling off completely. In such a case the restorer must strengthen the paint layer before he applies tissue-paper facing, otherwise the removal of the paper after consolidation would strip off the paint as well. Usually an adhesive brushed gently over the painted area will save the situation. Soluble nylon has become very popular for this purpose. It forms a tough protective layer over delicate pigments without producing any unwanted sheen on the surface, and being a fairly strong adhesive, holds firmly in place any flakes of paint that might have been in danger of breaking away.

Painted wood may often collect a stubbornly ingrained surface dirt. Paint is usually applied onto a white "ground" (a base layer) made of powdered chalk or gypsum. This sets the restorer another problem, for if he uses a cleaning fluid containing water, the ground will soften and the paint layer will disintegrate. One way around this danger is to use a special soap, which, instead of dissolving in water, dissolves in alcohol. This is then applied without damaging the strength of the ground.

But if the paint is in a very fragile state, even the gentlest brush strokes can destroy rather than clean. Just such a problem as this confronted a restorer faced with the task of cleaning some ancient Egyptian wooden slabs painted with marvelous descriptions of people and events of 3,000 years ago. The paint was so delicate that there could be no question of rubbing or brushing it. The restorer therefore decided to try cleaning it with a kind of silicone rubber that looks and

A conservator working in the Fortezza di Basso in Florence. Here he is cutting away worm-eaten and rotten parts of a wooden support for a painting, before grafting in a new piece of timber and consolidating the whole.

feels like "silly putty," but is rather more tacky. He gently rolled a small piece of it over chosen areas of the wooden slabs, periodically kneading it between his hands to produce a fresh, clean surface. The "putty" took up the ingrained dirt, leaving the paint clean and unharmed.

Sir Leonard Woolley, the discoverer of the famous silver lyre, spent about 12 years excavating the ruins of the ancient city of Ur. Apart from finding hundreds of fascinating treasures—including those from the Great Death Pit—he uncovered a large number of delicately inscribed clay tablets. But 4,000 years ago in Ur clay tablets were rarely fired in kilns to make them permanently hard. Most had merely been dried in the sun. The specimens Woolley found were therefore extremely fragile and powdery. Even worse, over the centuries they had become encrusted with salts absorbed from the surrounding soil. Many inscriptions were completely hidden. The problem Woolley faced was that if he tried to brush the unbaked tablets clean, he would almost certainly crumble the delicate inscriptions to dust.

How, then, could he clean the tablets? Instead of racking his brains for a way to remove the crust of salts directly, he hit upon a way of converting the tablets from their fragile state to a hard, durable one. First, he built an oil-fired kiln on the site. Then any lump of clay that looked like an encrusted tablet was placed in a metal box packed with clean sand and fired in the kiln, just as a potter fires a clay vase. The high temperatures in the kiln converted the unbaked clay to rock-hard terracotta— unglazed, reddish-yellow pottery. Having done this Woolley could give the tablets a vigorous scrub to remove the incrustations without endangering the inscriptions.

This simple but effective technique that Woolley devised at the site of his finds is still used in museum laboratories today.

With a seriously damaged panel painting, not only must all the wood be removed before effecting a transfer, but also the gesso ground must be meticulously scraped away. This calls for a very light touch—surgeons' scalpels and small knives being used. Finally (right), the conservator will be left with just the paint film on the facing of tissue, which would have been applied before the operation was begun. The picture shows the back of the artist's original painting.

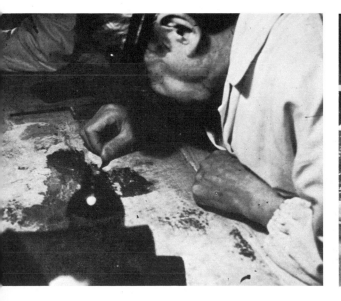

Nowadays, experts turn to all kinds of sophisticated chemical and physical techniques to analyze most of the clay objects that come their way. But when faced with fragile, sun-baked tablets, the method they use is essentially the same as Woolley's.

While the scribes of Ur told the story of their world on clay tablets, the Egyptians developed a crude form of paper from papyrus, the paper reed or paper rush. This aquatic plant was formerly abundant in Egypt, and still grows abundantly in many African rivers. Papyrus, widely cultivated in the Nile Delta in ancient times, was used for a variety of purposes. The head provided garlands for the shrines of gods; the wood was utilized for making various utensils as well as for fuel; the pith was an article of food, eaten both raw and cooked. The stem was used for making boats, sails, matting, cords, and cloth, but above all else for writing material. Early records tell of the widespread use of such writing material, and papyrus rolls are shown in ancient Egyptian wall-paintings.

The method of making papyrus rolls was as follows. With a sharp knife the stem of the plant was cut into longitudinal strips, those from the center of the stem were the broadest and best. The strips were now laid side by side on a board, each touching or slightly overlapping the next, until they made up the required width. Then another layer of shorter strips was placed across them at right angles. Next, after being well soaked with water, the whole sheet was hammered to weld it together, and placed in the sun to dry. Finally, any roughness was polished away with a smooth shell or piece of ivory. To form a roll, several sheets were joined together with paste. On this writing material the scribes would paint delicate picture-writing called *hieroglyphics*, recording deeds, agreements, inventories, and proclamations. Over the years archaeologists working among the ruins of ancient Egyptian temples and palaces or in the gloom of royal burial chambers, have discovered thousands of papyrus scrolls. But they can rarely read them right away. Millennia of burial in hot, arid conditions usually leave the scrolls brittle and extremely fragile. The archaeologist must hand them over to the restorer before he can hope to learn what secrets they hold.

The restorer carefully moistens the brittle scroll to revive some of its flexibility and begins to unroll it, a short length at a time. As he unrolls each length, he covers it with dry blotting paper and weighs it down with a sheet of glass. Throughout the operation the unrolled portion of the scroll is kept moist, to maintain the all-important flexibility.

Very often the papyrus has been torn or broken, and needs some expert first aid. The restorer uses small pieces of goldbeater's skin (a prepared animal membrane), with flour paste or some other water-soluble adhesive for the repair work. But in some cases, when the scroll is so brittle that moistening is

This copy of an Egyptian wall painting shows papyrus growing in the marshes. The stem of this plant was used by the Egyptians to make a writing material. Thousands of papyrus scrolls have been discovered in Egyptian tombs, but they must be treated by special methods before they can be unrolled and then deciphered.

useless, he actually breaks the scroll into small fragments. These are eventually reassembled as a flat manuscript.

In the late 1940s and early 1950s many ancient writings of quite a different kind were discovered in caves around Qumran, near the northwestern shores of the Dead Sea. They were manuscripts and fragments of manuscripts that had once belonged to the library of a community of Essenes, a Jewish religious brotherhood that flourished at the time of Jesus Christ. The Essenes led a hard disciplined life. Some branches of the sect did not marry and kept up their numbers by adopting children. Any profit they made from their labor went into a common purse, from which all expenses were paid. Some biblical scholars speculate that John the Baptist may have been adopted by the Essenes when a young boy. This would certainly be a logical reason for his being in the desert at such an early age.

The library of sacred books the Essenes built up meant much to them, and it is likely that in the troubled times when the Jews revolted against Roman rule they hid their precious manuscripts in caves, probably hoping to recover them when more peaceful times returned. But the chance never came, and the writings lay hidden for close on 1900 years. Then they

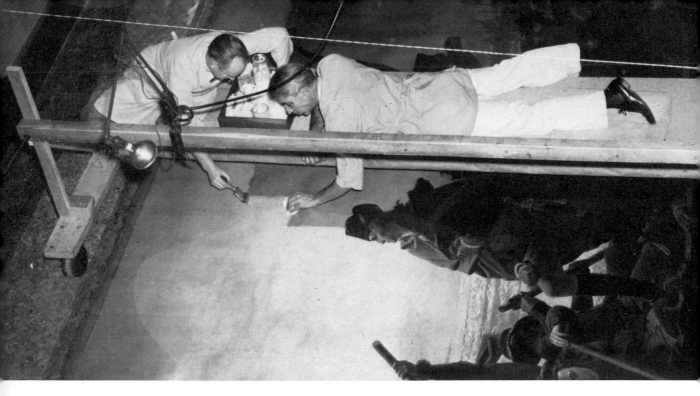

Grime and discolored varnish are removed from *Washington Crossing the Delaware* by men working on a specially constructed, 15-foot-long elevated platform.

were at last brought to light and became known throughout the world as the Dead Sea Scrolls. They include a copy of the Book of Leviticus in Palaeo-Hebrew script, a large Psalms Scroll, all the books of the Hebrew canon except Esther, the great Isaiah Scroll, and a scroll of Thanksgiving hymns.

But the scrolls were of leather and parchment (which is also made from animal skins), and after their long cave burial they were in no state to be read the moment they were found. In some cases parchment scrolls bearing writings had been wrapped in thicker leather, which had decomposed into a syrupy black substance that clung to the scrolls, making them almost impossible to unroll. When the restorers tried to moisten it, it simply became more glue-like. Eventually they devised a plan to freeze and moisten the scrolls alternately. By this means they loosened the grip of the decomposed leather. Then, using a fine scalpel to pry the layers free, they finally unrolled the scrolls.

Despite all these near-miracles of the restorer's art, the most impressive works of restoration are those that involve the cleaning of old paintings. It is easy to see why. Take the example of *Bacchus and Ariadne* by the great Italian painter Titian. The painting was one of the 30 or so works that founded the National Gallery's collection in London, in the 1800s. In 1967 restorers at the gallery decided not only to clean the picture but also to remove a past relining canvas and put the painting onto a panel for safer keeping. The job took two years and the effect was electrifying. It was as though Titian had only just walked away from his completed canvas. The pigments had come back to life. The reds were suddenly

Right: Painting restorers at work in the laboratory of the Institut Royal du Patrimoine Artistique, in Brussels.

68

Right: A specialist at work separating strips of papyrus. After being moistened, the scrolls are unrolled a bit at a time, covered with blotting paper, and then weighed down with glass as shown here.

red again. The blues were clear and bright.

To talk of "cleaning" a painting is somewhat misleading. What it really means is removing from the top of the paint the layers of old varnish that have darkened and cracked over the years. It is rather like stripping off a single layer of skin without harming the one beneath. The job demands tremendous patience, skill, and experience.

The restorer needs to have not only chemical knowledge, but also an understanding of the history of art, in order to adapt his methods to the techniques and materials used by the different painters. The essential step is to choose a solvent that will completely remove the varnish without affecting the paint. Only a small area of the painting can be tackled at a time. A constant watch must be kept for the first signs of crumbling or dissolving paint. Then, when the cleaning is at last finished, a fresh coat of varnish is applied. The newest kinds, made with synthetic resins, are far less likely to darken, yellow, bloom (mist over), or crack as the centuries go by than were the old natural resin varnishes. Further, they can normally be removed with far milder solvents than are needed for the old natural resin varnishes.

Most oil paintings are a complex sandwich of different materials. The sandwich begins with a base, or support, such as wood or canvas. The support is usually treated with a glue-like substance called *size* to make it nonabsorbent. A coat of white lead or similar substance, known as *primer*, goes on over the size as a basic ground on which to paint. On top of the primer many artists have applied a coat of thin pigment called *imprimatura*, and some have actually used this layer as part of the final painting. For example, John Constable, the British landscape artist of the 1800s, often left a red ocher imprimatura showing through in areas of shade. Over the imprimatura go two, three, or more layers of paint. Finally, on top of this, the artist uses one or more layers of protective varnish or wax. European artists of the 1400s and 1500s often used wood panels as supports. These were first covered with a layer of *gesso*, which was usually made of powdered gypsum or chalk, mixed with glue or size. Rabbit-skin glue was most popular because it was almost colorless, and not so liable to crack as hoof or fish glues. The hardened gesso on the wooden support provided an excellent painting surface. Including the gesso ground, a picture painted in this way may be made up of as many as eight distinct layers.

Before any restorer can begin work on a painting, he must have a thorough understanding of its complex layered structure. In the past, one of the worst dangers to paintings was the ignorance of would-be restorers. Their mishandling caused huge paint losses, which, all too often, were clumsily replaced. Heavy layers of dark yellow-brown "restoring" varnishes dulled and obscured original colors. In the 1800s it was even fashionable to coat paintings with this type of varnish to give an impression of great age.

The artists themselves sometimes complicated matters as well. Some used what are now called *fugitive pigments*—pigments that fade or change greatly with time. And in the 1700s many artists, including the great British portrait painter Sir Joshua Reynolds, first President of the Royal Academy, used bitumen as a pigment. Although the rich crimson-brown it produces is very tempting to artists and extremely attractive at first, the really destructive side of bitumen's character soon shows up. It "bleeds" or seeps into neighboring colors, and its drying time is unpredictable. Sometimes it will run down the face of the picture even after months of apparently normal drying. Finally, when it does dry, it produces a heavy pattern of cracks in the paint surface, and even lumps nearly a quarter of an inch thick. When the modern restorer goes to work he often has to deal with all these complications as well as with the normal batterings produced by the environment.

He starts with the canvas, paper, card, or wood support for the painting's ground. If the support is of canvas and has deteriorated, he attaches a new canvas to the back of the old one with what is called a *vacuum hot-table*. An adhesive, made of *beeswax* and *damar resin*, is melted on the electrically heated bed of the table. The two canvases are drawn together by the force of a vacuum, and the adhesive welds them firmly to one another, also impregnating the ground and paint layers. In the case of wooden supports the problems may be

Above: This portrait of *Mrs. Payne and Her Daughters* by Sir Joshua Reynolds lost one member of the family sometime between 1883 and 1908.
Right: During cleaning in 1935, another picture restorer discovered Mrs. Payne beneath the blue sky and restored her to her place beside the piano.

different. Suppose, in the first place, the wood has only been weakened, by insect attack for instance. All the restorer needs to do is to strengthen the existing wood while protecting the painting itself, as he goes about the job. The painting surface is covered with a facing of tissue-paper while the worm-eaten wood is impregnated with a hot wax from the back. Sometimes, however, the wood support has become completely rotten. The only answer then is to replace the wood. This operation, referred to as a "transfer," is not nearly such a

The cleaning of prints and drawings after the Florence floods posed many problems for the conservators. Care in the use of solvents and cleaning agents was very necessary, as they could have affected the inks and media originally used.

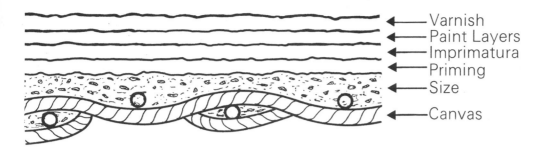

Varnish
Paint Layers
Imprimatura
Priming
Size
Canvas

straightforward job as the relining of a canvas support. It means transferring the painting itself from its original support to a new one. The restorer does this by slowly removing the wood, working from the back of the support through toward the gesso on which the painting lies. But as in the procedure for strengthening a partially damaged support, his first concern is for the painting itself. So he begins by applying a facing of tissue paper to the painting, then lays it face down on a soft, flat support. A set of clamps hold it firmly in place.

Now the restorer starts the tricky job. The kinds of tools and the way they are used will be determined by the condition and thickness of the particular wood panel. The first layers of wood are rasped away with a coarse file. But in every case, as the back of the priming or gesso ground is approached, the restorer turns to the finest instruments—tiny scrapers or surgical scalpels. At times the gesso ground itself may have decomposed and this, too, will have to be removed. A wrong move will punch a hole in the precious paint film. When this final procedure has been carried out satisfactorily, a strong new support will be added.

Drawings, watercolors, and prints on sized paper are particularly vulnerable to dampness. The worst problem that it produces is *foxing*—ugly brown stains that may start as a pinprick and spread to deface the whole work.

Foxing is caused by fungus taking root in the paper fibers or in the material used for sizing. When it has not gone very far, the restorer deals with it by gently brushing a mixture of spirit and a powerful bleach, hydrogen peroxide, onto the affected areas. He leaves the mixture for a few minutes and then rinses it off with distilled water. The treatment, if handled properly, removes the fungus stains without damaging the picture. In more extreme cases the whole work must be immersed in a bleaching fluid.

In the past 20 or so years the restoration of museum objects and works of art has made rapid strides. Each object, however badly wrecked or decayed, brings a challenge to the restorer, and it is seldom that he will have to concede defeat. Yet there is still room for more research to prepare for problems that will almost certainly arise with our future environment.

A diagram of a cross section of a painting. The circles and wavy lines represent the threads of the canvas. The priming coat, usually of white lead, provides an appropriate surface on which to paint. In addition, some painters apply *imprimatura,* a thin coat of pigment, which may show through the finished work.

An honest reproduction, such as the armorial plate *(left)* made by Samson and Co. in Paris in the 1800s, can be passed off as an original by removing the identifying mark on the back. At right is a: A Chinese import of the 1700s—the sort of object that inspired Samson's work.

Fakes & Forgers

In the spring of 1945 World War II ended with Europe in chaos. Bombings, devastation, and the displaced populations left in their wake a scene that would take years to unravel. During the six years Europe had lain in the shadows of war, there had been lootings and transfers of works of art on a scale hardly equaled before. Now that hostilities had ceased, organizations both international and national set about the immense task of trying to get everybody and everything back to where it really belonged. Suddenly, out of this scene of turmoil and effort, a most extraordinary story of art forgery was to emerge. Indeed, the forger supreme was uncovered.

The Dutch commissioners responsible for restoring the art of the Netherlands to its rightful owners came up with a strange discovery. Herman Göring, one of the Nazi leaders, had ruthlessly made for himself a collection of works of art that must have compared with any in history. As the experts slowly cataloged and examined this hoard, they came across what seemed to be a fine example of the work of Jan Vermeer, one of the great Dutch painters of the 1600s. What really shook them was that the picture, entitled *Christ and the Adulteress*, had not previously been known as an existing work by the master. The initial astonishment of the commissioners soon gave way to puzzlement and then anger. How had a painting from the brush of such a rare artist been kept from the Dutch people? How had it found its way into the hands of one of their archenemies?

The Dutch police force immediately mounted a full-scale investigation. After months of work and sifting through records they found that the man who had sold the picture was Han van Meegeren, an Amsterdam painter. They arrested him on a charge of "collaboration with the enemy," the punishment for which, if the crime were proved, would be a very heavy prison sentence.

Van Meegeren at first angrily denied the charge, claiming that he had not known that Göring was the ultimate buyer. He said he had dealt entirely through an agent and had never at any time been told the buyer's identity. Van Meegeren's story, however, was not believed, and he was taken to jail. There, quite suddenly, he stopped protesting. Even when fiercely

questioned he maintained a stubborn silence. Once the cell door closed on him, it seemed that he had resolved never to answer the charge. But six weeks later he broke down. Without any warning he turned on his inquisitors.

"Fools!" he shouted. "You are fools like the rest of them! I sold no great national treasure—I painted it myself!"

The police officers stared in amazement as Van Meegeren went on to list as his own a number of paintings previously acclaimed by experts as masterpieces not only by Vermeer, but also by Frans Hals, Pieter de Hooch, and other famous Dutch artists of the same period.

The initial reaction of the police and the art experts was disbelief: the man was obviously trying to avoid punishment by telling a stupid lie. Van Meegeren was not taken seriously until he had actually painted another "Vermeer," *The Young Christ,* before witnesses. The affair caused a public sensation, for Van Meegeren had made fools of many highly respected critics (which had been one of his intentions). But to complicate matters he had not, in the strict sense of the word, forged anything but a master's signature. After all, he had never copied another painting, but simply worked in the same style as a master.

With great skill he had cunningly imitated the style of Vermeer and had painted works that the experts might be expected to think would turn up one day. Besides being a master of techniques, the wily Van Meegeren was also a student of art history. He knew that most of the Dutch painters of Vermeer's time had painted at least some New Testament scenes. But if Vermeer had followed the trend of his time, his biblical paintings had either been lost or destroyed—with the exception of one early work. Yet the art experts hoped more might be discovered. Indeed, Van Meegeren "discovered" them for the world of art, and, by providing what the experts were ready to accept, diverted

Two of the Van Meegeren forgeries of religious subjects aiming at the manner of Vermeer. Above is a detail from *The Last Supper* and at left *Isaac Blessing Jacob.* In the latter can be seen the distinctive white ewer that appears in several of Van Meegeren's forgeries, including the notorious *Supper at Emmaus.*

suspicion. Was he to be tried for the signatures or the paintings? It was an interesting legal question, and, in fact, he was eventually tried for both.

How had Van Meegeren been able to deceive so many experts? Before his confession none of his paintings had been subjected to any thorough scientific examination. There had been a rather superficial study by microscope and spectroscope. Some tests for the resistance of paints to alcohol and other solvents and some analysis of colors had been carried out. But because the experts were ready to accept the paintings as the missing part of Vermeer's work, none of these tests had gone far enough, so that the findings seemed insufficient to raise suspicion. The art experts had relied on their experience and their emotions. The trained human eye may often be the reason for the start of an investigation into a forgery, but it should never be relied upon alone to say whether a picture or an object is genuine or false.

In 1937 an aged and respected critic, Abraham Bredius, one of the outstanding art experts and critics of the time, certified the first of the forgeries of Van Meegeren as a Vermeer. This picture was *Christ's Supper at Emmaus,* and Bredius wrote an effusive article for the internationally-read journal of art, *The Burlington Magazine,* in which he extolled the quality of the painting and proclaimed its authenticity. In the same context it is of interest to note that when the Duveen Brothers, a firm of art dealers in New York, sent a query to Europe about this painting of *Christ's Supper at Emmaus,* their Paris representative replied with the following cable, dated October 4, 1937: "SEEN TODAY AT BANK LARGE VERMEER ABOUT FOUR FEET BY THREE CHRIST'S SUPPER AT EMMAUS SUPPOSED BELONG PRIVATE FAMILY CERTIFIED BY BREDIUS WHO WRITING ARTICLE BURLINGTON MAGAZINE NOVEMBER STOP PRICE POUNDS NINETY THOUSAND STOP PICTURE ROTTEN FAKE."

Van Meegeren painting *The Young Christ* after his arrest in May, 1945. Charged with having sold Vermeers to the Nazis, he insisted that he had painted the pictures himself, but was not believed by his inquisitors until he painted this other, final forgery before their eyes.

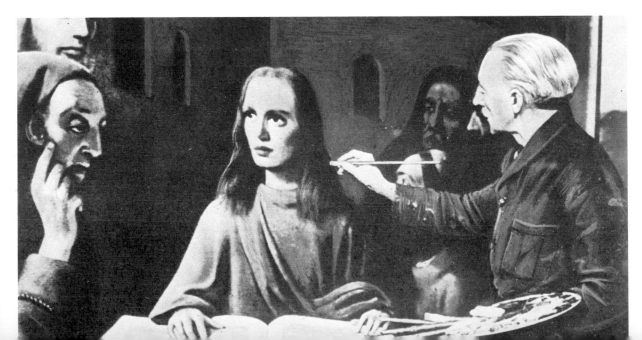

Once alerted, modern technologists could probably have revealed the forgeries. This, however, is by no means certain, for Van Meegeren had taken immense pains to escape detection.

The surface—or skin—of an oil painting dries after only a few days. But the complete drying and hardening process, especially where the paint is thick, can take up to 50 years. Knowing this, Van Meegeren experimented with a number of sample paintings to see how he could best reproduce the authentic effect of old paint that had been drying for three centuries or so. First he tried heating to different temperatures, but this resulted in blistering and discoloration. Then he turned to a more sophisticated technique. He had heard of a hard material known as Bakelite, made from two chemicals called phenol and formaldehyde, that had been developed in the United States in 1908. It struck him that if these two chemicals produced a hard material like Bakelite they might also harden his paints in just the way he wanted. Over the next two years Van Meegeren worked at this idea, and eventually perfected a technique of artificial aging. With the addition of just the right amount of phenol and formaldehyde he could achieve a hardening of his paints that was authentic enough to fool the experts.

Van Meegeren's work on pigments was no less painstaking. He knew that modern artificial pigments would not pass even the most casual chemical analysis. Jan Vermeer's favorite blue was genuine ultramarine (which is extracted from the semiprecious stone called Lapis Lazuli). In one of his statements to the police Van Meegeren said he had obtained genuine ultramarine "in the early part of 1931" from Winsor & Newton, one of the leading London dealers in artists' supplies, who confirmed that four separate orders for ultramarine, totaling 12½ ounces, had been made. The pigment is so very expensive and so rarely asked for that it was assumed that Van Meegeren was the customer on each occasion, though his name did not appear in the firms' records. It is possible that Van Meegeren may have done some final grinding of the ultramarine itself. After having gone to the expense of procuring the real pigment, it is extraordinary that in two of his fakes the presence was detected of some cobalt blue, a pigment which was not discovered until 1802.

Yet, even today, there is argument as to whether, if the paintings had been subjected to thorough scientific examination in the first place, the analysts could have broken through the deception and recognized all the forgeries.

In collecting evidence for the case against Van Meegeren scientists soon found telltale traces of phenol and formaldehyde in the paint. During the examination they also found that there were residues of black ink in the crackled varnish on top of the paint. This had been put into the cracks to imitate the look of normal dirt in the cracked surface of an old picture. But the point is that they applied the appropriate tests to identify these chemicals only after Van Meegeren had described the hardening technique he had used. If the scientists had not known what to look for, it is unlikely that they would have stumbled on the evidence.

The truth is that only a twist of fate—Göring's acquisition of *Christ and the Adulteress*—exposed Van Meegeren. The damning evidence presented at his trial was assembled only after his confession. The master forger was eventually sentenced to just a year's imprisonment. But on December 29, 1947, a bare month after the sentence had been passed on him, Han van Meeregen died.

Much of the interest in this case centers on the reason as to why Van Meegeren ever started faking. Possibly the initial reason was psychological. What was his history? Han van Meegeren was born in 1889 in Deventer, Holland. His schoolmaster father, Henricus, was a very strict man. Henricus was 40 when he married, and Han was the second son. Han could remember that so puritan was his early life that he was not allowed even to speak in his father's presence unless he had first been spoken to.

In High School Han was taught drawing and painting by Bartus Korteling, an artist and teacher who was to become a lifelong friend. Although he soon showed himself to have considerable talent and began to win awards, his father stubbornly opposed any thought of an artistic career. The family was now in a perpetual state of discord, as father and son were completely out of sympathy with each other. Nevertheless, encouraged by Korteling's teaching and sympathy, Han persevered. In 1907, when he was 18, his father was at last forced to recognize his talent, and sent Han to Delft to study architecture at the Institute of Technology. His interest in painting never flagged, so while studying architecture he set out to win the gold medal that was awarded every five years for the best painting from a student by the Institute of Technology. This he did, and by 1913 began to sell his works. One watercolor sold for almost $500, a high figure even for an established painter of that time.

Seen here modeling some figures in clay, Alceo Dossena worked with remarkable speed and skill. His versatile talent produced sculpture in the style of various periods—such as the "Renaissance" bas-relief *Madonna and Child (right)*. For such work he received a few *lire* from dealers—who would pass it off as authentic at an enormous profit.

Success as an artist in his own right began to come to him. In 1914 he moved to The Hague, where his drawings, watercolors, and portraits drew praise from the social set. On the day Britain declared war on Germany, August 4, 1914, Han received his degree from The Hague Academy of Art. Later he was offered a professorship at the Academy, but he turned it down. The critics gave him good notices for his work, and he found himself in demand not only for paintings, but also for lessons. His famous picture *Deer,* which is reported to have been reproduced more than any other in Holland, was done as a demonstration during one of his classes.

In 1922 Van Meegeren organized a one-man exhibition of biblical paintings in The Hague and sold every one. Success, and the money that went with it opened new vistas for Han. Gradually, however, the praise of the critics began to flag, and this brought out a bitter trait in Han's character. He later said that one of the reasons for his taking up forgery was the failure of his countrymen to recognize his genius.

In the early 1930s, Han left Holland and moved to the Riviera, settling finally in Nice. He stated that about this time his capital was in the neighborhood of £15,000, which he earned by painting portraits of rich American and British tourists. When World War II broke out in 1939 he returned to Holland, where according to reports he lived in some considerable style throughout the war, a fact that can be

THE FORGERIES SOLD BY VAN MEEGEREN

Vermeer

	Guilders	Dollars	Sterling *
Christ at Emmaus	520,000	290,000	58,000
Christ's Head (a study)	550,000	264,000	61,000
The Last Supper	1,600,000	712,000	178,000
Isaac Blessing Jacob	1,270,000	564,000	141,000
The Washing of Christ's Feet	1,300,000	576,000	144,000
Christ and the Adulteress	1,650,000	495,000	183,000
de Hooch			
The Card Players	290,000	128,000	32,000
A Drinking Party	220,000	97,000	24,000
	7,400,000	3,126,000	821,000

These figurines are all copies of 18th-century English pieces. The lamb was copied by Samson of Paris from a Derby original. The goldfinch, also supposedly Derby, is a 20th-century forgery; and the cat, derived from a Staffordshire pottery figure, was forged as recently as 1968.

Bought in 1937 for the Boymans Museum, Amsterdam, paid for by the state, and the Rembrandt Society

Bought in 1941, by D. G. van Beuningen and traded in to Hoogendjuk, the art dealer, in part payment for The Last Supper

Bought in 1941 by D. G. van Beuningen, of Rotterdam

Bought in 1942 by W. van der Vorm, of Rotterdam

Bought by the Dutch State

Bought by Göring, 1943

Bought by D. G. van Beuningen about 1939

Bought by W. van der Vorm about 1940

✱Dollar and Sterling equivalents correct for time of purchase in each case

understood from the sale prices of his faked Dutch masters.

As a final indication of the strange quirks of his character, it is recorded that when Van Meegeren was asked by the judge during his trial to comment on the work of scientists who had investigated the whole affair, he replied sarcastically: "I find this work excellent. Indeed it is phenomenal. It will never be possible to get away with forgery again. To me, such work seems much more clever than—for example—the painting of *Christ's Supper at Emmaus.*"

Legally, the strange thing is that copying or imitating works of art is not in itself a crime of forgery even if the copies are sold. The crime of forgery is committed only when the forger or his associates "utter the forgery"—in legal language this means when they make an attempt to sell or dispose of the copy as a genuine work of art.

The prime cause that drives most forgers is the old law of supply and demand. The scarcer the genuine article becomes, the higher sale prices are hoisted. So is the stage set for the forger who can come in to satisfy the needs of the museum, the gallery, or the private collector. Sometimes, as with Van Meegeren, the desire for quick wealth may be coupled with a desire to prove equal technical and artistic skill with an acknowledged genius. The situation is further complicated, because throughout history numerous copies of paintings, sculpture, and other objects have been made. In the first instance this is probably done in all innocence, but after the works have changed hands a few times individuals start to add spurious attributions and signatures, so that an innocently made copy becomes a forgery.

The story of forging art is by no means confined to the 20th century. There are two anecdotes linking one of the world's greatest masters with forgery. Giorgio Vasari, an historian, architect, and painter of the 1500s, records that when Michelangelo was studying in the studio of his teacher Ghirlandaio "there he was given a drawing of a head to copy, which he did with such skill that his master took for the original the copy which Michelangelo returned to him until he found the boy rejoicing over his success with one of his companions. Afterwards many people compared the two sheets without finding any difference between them. For, in addition to the perfect rendering of the original design, Michelangelo had been careful to smoke the paper of his copy in order to make it look as old as its model." At another time the young Michelangelo is reported to have made a perfect copy of an early Greek statue, *Cupid Asleep*. To give this work an antique appearance, he buried it in the damp earth, and later it was sold in Rome in 1496 as a piece of classical sculpture.

During the Renaissance there was a mania for collecting that is probably equaled only today. Vasari also tells of many incidents of well-known artists producing copies of the antique, and also of the production of pastiches in which parts of several original works were taken and put together. Legal history shows that the career of the forger is one of considerable risk. In 1562, under English law, the forging of a signature could be punished by: being fined, standing in the pillory, having both ears cut off and the nostrils slit and seared, forfeiting one's land, and perpetual imprisonment. By 1634 forgery had been made a capital offense. In the United States today conviction for forgery usually results in long terms of imprisonment.

Although much forgery is quite obviously conceived and carried out in extreme secrecy, it does appear to have something in common with other crimes, in that, if there is a lot of publicity in the papers and on the television following the discovery of a fake, shortly afterwards a veritable rash breaks out. How much forgery is actually being carried on today is impossible even to guess at.

The problem for the director of a museum or gallery is complicated when advising on purchases. It is not his own money that he is laying out, but often huge sums from public resources and private subscriptions. He may have behind him the services of a laboratory and experts, but the sheer variety of objects being collected acts on the forger's side. Within the last few years museum authorities have met attempts to pass off not only paintings, which seem to be always favorites, but also articles as assorted as Egyptian bronze cats, pieces of tapestry, ceramics, and early Roman glass figures. There is a very high demand for early American art. Many an unwary traveler in Mexico and Central America has bought a bit of pre-Columbian pottery that is hardly cool from its firing.

During the past ten years the Metropolitan Museum of Art in New York, the British Museum, the Ashmolean Museum at Oxford, as well as other museums and private collectors in the United States and Europe bought objects they thought to have been genuine Neolithic ceramics excavated at Hacilar in Turkey. This New Stone Age site was discovered in 1956, and genuine painted-pottery vessels and figures found there have been dated back to 5500 B.C. It was, however, not long before some of the objects from the site came under suspicion. Various authorities began to raise doubts on the basis of style and technique. Then the scientists took a hand. Thermoluminescent dating techniques (see Chapter 3) quickly showed that many of the pieces were fakes of recent origin.

In 1971 Turkish police arrested a man and charged him with forging Neolithic ceramics. It seems that this *entrepreneur* had taken advantage of the world demand for this type of antiquity, and infiltrated his fakes into the supply line.

Keepers of coin and medal departments need to be on the look out for a "Billie and Charlie." This is a small forged medal that takes its name from two characters who earned a chancy living mudraking in the Pool of London in the late 19th century. One day they had seen a workman dredge up a hoard of pilgrim medals that had originally been made to be given to visitors to the Holy Land and other sacred places. When they had found that these medals were sought after by collectors and would fetch a good price, Billy and Charlie put their heads together. They gave up their mudraking and started to produce a large number of pilgrim medals. During the hours of darkness, they would put them into the tidal mud of the Pool of London, and then at the next low tide excavate them with a certain degree of publicity. For a time Billy and Charlie lived well from their enterprise, but at last some dealers became suspicious. However, an investigation conducted by expert witnesses cleared the medals and they were declared absolutely genuine. Encouraged by this, the enterprising pair went into mass production and their profit soared. Unfortunately for them, a scholar somewhat more able than the earlier experts pointed out a slight oversight in their productions. Around the edges of the medals there were

A modern forgery purporting to be by El Greco. X-ray examination showed clearly that there is another painting of quite a different subject underneath. The second photograph shows where the conservator has carefully removed part of the later painting to disclose in detail an area of the first work.

strange oriental characters that appeared to be Arabic, but were in fact just nonsense. Besides this, most of the medals were dated around the 11th century, and the scholar pointed out that Arabic was not known in Europe until the 13th century. The police closed in on the secret workshop. Billy and Charlie had had their day.

Careful market research enables the potential forger to profit from trends in art collecting. Currently there has been an underground factory in Spain producing excellent imitations of old armor. Violins purporting to be genuine examples of the work of Stradivarius are seeping into the market. These instruments—many carrying a small label reading "Antonius Stradivarius Cremonensis"—are now being produced in East Germany and France. In the 1930s, however, a number came from Czechoslovakia. It is impossible to tell how many of these fakes are around. This fact applies to the whole field of forgeries, partly because an individual, having paid out a lot of money for one, is often loath to admit he has been duped.

Considerable confusion can also arise for the art historian and collector when there is an instance of a family of artists

One of the biggest art disputes of this century arose over this wax bust of *Flora,* attributed to Leonardo da Vinci. Some experts claimed that the bust is a 19th-century forgery. Even microchemical analysis of the pigments used to paint the bust failed to produce conclusive evidence to support either side.

Above: This triptych, supposedly a work of the Sienese school of the 15th century, was discovered to be a forgery with the aid of X rays. The X-ray photograph (*left*) revealed the use of modern hinges and machine-made nails in the wood.

who all paint the same type of picture. A good example of this was found in the English family of Alken who produced sporting pictures and prints. The period of their production lasted from the time of Sefferin Alken (1717-1782), to that of Henry Gordon Alken, who died in 1894. Within that period of more than 100 years there were, besides these two, Samuel (the son of the original Sefferin) and four of his sons, Sam, George, Sefferin, and Henry, followed by two sons of this Henry, whom he christened Henry and Sefferin. The problem for the art historian can be sympathized with when it is known that all the Alkens painted in the same style and signed their pictures S. or H. Alken. The last Alken, who was actually christened Samuel Henry but called Henry Gordon, signed some of his pictures H. Alken, Junior, but at the same time did a grave injustice to his father not only by omitting the "Junior" in some cases but by sometimes deliberately forging and passing off his rather poor work as that of his father. Since he died as a pauper in a workhouse, he was obviously not very successful.

The Van Meegeren affair may have filled the newspapers, but seen in its correct context it is really only one recent bright highlight of an immense, worldwide, and historically age-old industry. In a much humbler vein was the case of the Roman terra-cotta lamps. The Pesaro Museum in Italy had one of the world's largest and most comprehensive collections of rare terra-cotta lamps. This had originally been assembled by the Italian antiquary Giovanni Battista Passeri

(1694-1780). Some 50 years ago an exhaustive investigation revealed that the Passeri collection was one of the greatest collections of fakes ever brought together. Practically all the more important pieces were declared as forgeries. In the collection there was an interesting lamp in the shape of a bull's head. An early expert had thought that lamps in this form were dedicated to Artemis Taurobolos. The forger, who must have done his homework, inscribed the horns with a dedication to the goddess Artemis. There was an error in the spelling that went unseen until the final investigation.

Pottery and porcelain have attracted the attention of the forger in practically all fields; notably that of Chinese ceramics, where the fakers have had an absolute heyday with the different periods and inscriptions. The first examples of pure Chinese porcelain, which were a development from stoneware, were produced during the T'ang Dynasty between A.D. 618 and 907. Many of these earliest pieces had beautiful green and creamy white glazes, making porcelain of this particular period one of the most popular for collectors in Europe and America. Yet despite the distinctive glazes, choosing a piece of T'ang porcelain can be full of pitfalls. There are imitations that date back to the year 1000. Quantities of T'ang forgeries were mass produced during the 18th and 19th centuries and are probably still being manufactured. Of the T'ang period it is the animals—the horses and camels—and the figures of ladies that are held to be most choice. However, when the earliest tomb figures—statues with grotesque faces—arrived

The celebrated bronze horse in the Metropolitan Museum, New York, which has aroused much controversy as to whether or not it is a 20th-century forgery. Supposedly of early Greek origin, the little horse—which stands just under 16 inches high—may yet be established as an original work of art.

in Europe just after the beginning of the 20th century they at once aroused interest. It was not long before wily forgers were onto the possibilities of moneymaking. And in 1912, when a Professor Yetts visited establishments which worked on T'ang ceramics, he wrote: "I visited a factory at Peking where along shelves stood hundreds of newly made figures. Comparison of these with the genuine originals which had served as patterns proved that certain modern replicas may defy detection." Here again it is style and aesthetic achievement that is most likely to give the lie to the fake. Many of the present-day T'ang figures that are coming off the production line have traces of modernity, particularly in the faces of the figures, or flights of imagination which diverge from the originals.

In 1918 art collectors were thrilled by the sudden appearance in some Paris showrooms of several hitherto unknown sculptures. Examples of Greek, Roman, Gothic, Renaissance, and other periods came to light. Rumors spread throughout the art-buying world that a major private collection was being disposed of item by item. Because buyers knew that the statues were coming from Italy, a few even made the suggestion that the Vatican was parting with some of its treasures.

As each statue appeared it was acclaimed as a work of ancient genius. In almost every case huge prices were paid for them. Soon many held pride of place in the world's most famous museums and private collections. In 1928 the truth

The demand for objects to fill the departments of museums and galleries has tempted forgers. The staff of these institutions need all their insight and scientific armory to screen out spurious objects. Here is a representation of Mars or an Etruscan warrior that is really a 20th-century production done in the style of the fifth century B.C.

was discovered. The statues "carved by artists of bygone centuries" were all the work of one Alceo Dossena, a 20th-century Italian stonemason.

Dossena was not a forger in the strict sense of the word. In the same way as Van Meegeren copied nothing, but painted in the styles characteristic of masters, so Dossena worked with uncanny skill in a number of ancient unmistakable manners. Unlike Van Meegeren, Dossena had no criminal streak. In fact he was cruelly exploited by "middle men." They commissioned Dossena to produce, say, a marble goddess in the Greek or Roman style. He would get on with the job with relish, enjoying every moment of his work. The middle men would then pay Dossena a few lire and secretly sell the statue at a huge profit as an authentic work.

Eventually Dossena heard about how he was being treated and announced to several art historians that he was the creator of the sculpture. He was derided. A simple Italian mason the creator of such glorious works of art? The idea was ridiculous! And besides, their reputations would never survive the shock if it were true.

In an endeavor to prove his claim Dossena allowed himself to be filmed at work. One of the team who worked on the filming later wrote: "Dossena worked so fast, and his results were always so unexpected that our camera could hardly keep up with him . . . . Half an hour later he had modelled in clay the figure of a goddess, some 60 centimetres high in the Attic style [that is, in the fashion of ancient Athens] . . . . "

But despite the sculptor's great skill the art world soon rejected Dossena. Works by him that had fetched monumental prices were suddenly devalued as no more than cheap fakes, while museum directors and private collectors ground their teeth in rage and shame. Scholars began to notice subtle flaws in style that they said should have been noticed before. Reputations suffered and finally people lost interest in this talented craftsman, who died in 1937, destitute in a pauper's hospital in Rome.

Another furore arose over a painted wax bust of *Flora,* which was purchased for the Berlin Museum in 1909 as an original by Leonardo da Vinci. In its time this produced almost as much publicity as the Van Meegeren affair, for many experts doubted that Leonardo had ever worked in wax. The battle of the experts was joined, and seldom has there been a display of more conflicting opinions from the top minds from each side. Wilhelm von Bode, Director of the Berlin Museum, was naturally lined up for the originality of the bust with Adolph Donath, art critic of the *Berliner Tageblatt*, and the scholar Edmund Hildebrandt. Against the work and declaring it to be a fake was Gustav Pauli of the

A laser beam is used here to detect a forgery. This portrait, allegedly painted in the 16th century, was found to contain zinc—which was not used in pigments until about 1820.

Kunsthalle, Hamburg. He came right out and said stylistically the work had the appearance of figures modeled of Queen Victoria. A writer in London's leading newspaper, *The Times,* expressed the opinion that the bust was the work of a little-known English sculptor, Richard Cockle Lucas (1800-1883). Lucas' son, who was still living, claimed he could remember having actually helped his father make the wax bust, preparing the model from a painting of the Leonardo school that a dealer had brought and asked him to copy. Another mystifying opinion was that the English art scholar E.V. Lucas in 1910 referred to the *Flora* as the work of his namesake sculptor and then 14 years later in *The Times* gave the opinion the work was an original.

Microchemical analysis was employed with tiny fragments of paint that were taken from an unimportant area of the bust. This analysis of pigment is a process that is often resorted to on a suspected forgery, since the results of the analysis can be compared with the accurate information as to which pigments were available at various periods of history. In the case of the

Flora the microscope revealed a translucent vehicle for the paints which had not been found after the 17th century and also traces of *archil,* a dye that comes from a lichen. But in the case of this particular dye such evidence is not conclusive, because it would be quite a simple matter for an intelligent forger to prepare archil-based colors of blue, violet, and red. In the case of the *Flora* things were complicated by one expert, Theodor von Frimmel, who in 1911 made the point that archil was certainly obtainable well after the end of the 16th century—that is, long after Leonardo's death.

The case of the wax *Flora* was further complicated when at the height of the controversy it was learned that another *Flora,* only this time of marble, not wax, had been bought for 50 lire by Alfredo Barsanti, an *entrepreneur* art dealer. He sold it as a Leonardo original to the Museum of Fine Arts, Boston, where it was described by L.D. Caskey as one of the great treasures of the collection. There is, however, still some doubt as to its authenticity.

On February 16, 1923, the Metropolitan Museum in New York bought a Greek bronze horse from a dealer in Paris. The date of its origin was thought to be between 480 and 470 B.C. Much scholarly writing lauded the work as a high point in the history of Greek art, and for years its authenticity was never questioned. Then in 1961 suspicion was aroused about the method of casting used to make the bronze. There was a hole in the mane presumably for harness, which seemed misplaced, because harness straps should tie right behind the ears, and in the forelock there was another deep hole of apparently uncertain purpose.

The scholars, who for years had accepted the horse as genuine, were naturally quite upset. An expert bronze founder in Brooklyn was consulted. He suggested the horse could have been cast around a core of sand and clay held in position by thin pieces of iron wire while the molten bronze was poured. The supposed forger could then have hidden the ends of the iron wires, which would not have melted, by cutting them back and putting in small bronze plugs to cover the holes. By using a magnet it was also possible to trace the direction of these internal iron wires supporting the core. Radiography was then used to show up the presence of these iron wires and the core.

The result of this technical examination seemed to indicate that the object was possibly a forgery, and for a time it was accepted as such by the Metropolitan Museum. However, the evidence was not regarded as conclusive by other scholars and scientists, and a subsequent, more detailed investigation of the composition of the alloy and other related factors seemed to point to the authenticity of the object. Conclusive elucidation of this problem is still awaited.

It may seem that the forger, if he is determined and astute and possesses considerable technical and historical knowledge, holds many strong cards in his hand. He will always have the

benefit of surprise, in that there is a fair chance that his first few efforts will slip in under the guard of dealer, collector, and expert.

What are the weapons that the art detective can rally to his aid? X-ray photography is a reliable and useful tool for examining all objects other than metal ones. In the case of paintings, it will disclose the various layers of the picture, and show up the artist's underpainting and drawing. X-ray photography will also show up the actual construction of a wood panel, and, as in the case of a Sienese triptych at the Courtauld Institute in London, immediately point to its falsity. An X-ray photograph of this work showed that the gilding and the painting had been put onto wood that was *already* eaten by worms, that the hinges were modern, and, more damning still, that machine-made nails had been used in the construction. X ray can further give some idea as to the chemical composition of a picture by the difference in tone values; for example, the trained eye can pick up a light tone value in the developed plate that will indicate the presence of lead. There is no doubt that from the forger's point of view the X rays have been in many ways one of the biggest snags. There have been actual cases in which the forger has attempted to cheat the X-ray camera by inserting a thin lead sheet between the priming and the support, but this is not a very wise course, because the very fact of a blank photograph coming through raises suspicion right away. X rays can also be useful to help determine the authenticity of ceramics and furniture. Here again an X-ray photograph would show up details underneath the surface glazes, patinas, or finishes that the eye would not see.

Ultraviolet light is a useful aid in showing up recent retouching or alterations, particularly in paintings. It will not uncover a fake, as would an X ray, but the use of ultraviolet will cause recent additions or re-paints to fluoresce. An infrared photograph will also give similar results but is less sensitive. But, as we saw in Chapter 2, infrared will show up details that may have become almost completely obliterated.

Another powerful tool in the examination of paintings and other works of art is the photomicrograph. When a camera is linked to a microscope and a high degree enlargement is made from the negative, an enormous amount of detail becomes visible that is completely invisible to the naked eye or even through an ordinary magnifying glass. Before the viewer's eyes the whole truth will be laid bare. The enlarged print of the photomicrograph will show every last detail of the brush strokes, the etcher's needle, the finish of a piece of furniture, the painted decoration on a piece of pottery. To defeat photomicrography, the forger is up against a much stiffer proposition even than with an X ray. His only hope is to

Part of the Ashley Library of forged first editions of works by authors such as Lord Byron and Wordsworth. Chemical analysis of the paper used by Wise showed that it was manufactured later than the dates of the supposed "first editions."

assimilate absolutely the entire working manner and technique of the artist he is faking.

In the examination of paintings, microchemical analysis can add much information that, when supplemented with the results of other investigations, often adds up to proof of falsity or of originality. With a hypodermic needle the investigator can take a tiny core from a painting. When it is ejected onto a microscope slide, the core, which is a cross section from paint surface to canvas, will show the varnish layers, paint, imprimatura, priming, and size or glue layers. The ability of this method to reveal the color layers is particularly important; for, as was mentioned earlier, there are definite facts as to when individual pigments were introduced. As technology improves so do the tools of the art detective.

An example of sophisticated, up-to-date methods of detection was the exposure of a forged painting in the Boston Museum of Fine Arts, where a painting of an old woman—supposedly from the 16th century—came under suspicion for certain matters of style. An analysis of the pigments was called for. In this case, however, rather than taking a hypodermic sample, the investigator vaporized a minute bit of paint with a laser beam. The vapor was then analyzed by means of a spectrograph as described in Chapter 2, and the constituents of the paint then assessed. The resulting spectrogram revealed the presence of zinc, a metallic element that was not used in making pigments until about 1820. The painting was a fake. The advantage of the laser technique in this instance was that it affected only a microscopic area of the paint surface, so that if the portrait had been genuine it would have suffered no serious harm in the process.

Chemical analysis led to the ultimate disgrace of one Thomas James Wise (1859-1937). The specialty of Wise was forging first editions of books by famous English writers, in particular Wordsworth, Ruskin, and Lord Byron. The scientists got to work only in the 1930s, when Wise had already made a reputation and a sizable fortune from his bookselling. In the laboratory, it came to light that Wise had used esparto grass paper in manufacturing books supposedly published before 1861. But it was not until 1861 that esparto was used in British papers. Similarly chemically pulped wood fiber was first used in Britain in 1874, but Wise's "first editions," supposedly published well before this date, showed signs of it.

One last trick of the forger is worth mentioning. This is to partially destroy and then quite honestly restore the work he has produced. If this process is cleverly carried out, it can be very misleading. For, in many cases, the mere fact of evident restoration is disarming and almost gives a feeling of authenticity. But the deception is likely to fall apart in the laboratory.

Disaster

At intervals in history nature has boiled up and wrecked not just a single work of art but a whole city. In a few hours its life, its culture, its buildings have been reduced to unrecognizable mockeries of their original splendor. Faced by total destruction, a solitary restorer or even a group may nearly despair at the immensity of the task. First the archaeologists may have to do their work of excavation before the restorers can begin.

The year was A.D. 63. Pompeii, the ancient Roman city of

The body of a Pompeiian
citizen who failed to escape
the avalanche of volcanic ash
that destroyed the city in
A.D. 79. The ash preserved
the bodies of many such
victims, giving us a vivid,
tangible record of an ancient
tragedy.

Campania lying just above the instep of the Italian boot, was
suddenly and violently shaken by an earthquake that either
destroyed or so seriously damaged the town that most of it
needed rebuilding. From existing remains we can see that the
Pompeiians were still working on the task in A.D. 79, when
once again the earth shook. This time it was not an earthquake,
but worse. Vesuvius, the great volcano that loomed up beside
the city, had burst into eruption. The moment must have been
one of terror as the skies filled with flying fire and dense

clouds of fumes, smoke, and cinders. Vesuvius spewed out millions of tons of ash, burying not only Pompeii but also the nearby town of Herculaneum where the volcanic ash piled up to a depth of up to 80 feet.

In a few short hours two cities quite simply ceased to exist— they were gone from their time. Yet in a horrific manner this catastrophic inundation was to preserve almost intact a record of the life that was so suddenly scorched out. Bodies came to light caught in their last struggles for survival, and many of the things the people used in their daily life have been found in the position of their last use, held safe in their deadly packing.

Gradually Pompeii and Herculaneum were forgotten. For nearly 2,000 years farmers laid out vineyards and tilled the fertile volcanic soil that covered the remains of these two cities. Then in 1738, the Queen of Naples, following the vogue of the wealthy for decorating their gardens with antique statues, heard a rumor that statues of the kind she wanted were being dug out of the ground near the base of Vesuvius. She set diggers to work who uncovered not only statues, but, much to their amazement, the first hint of a buried city. It was not until 1763, however, that systematic excavation was commenced, and although this was carried on during the 18th century it was not until the 19th that it became thoroughly organized in a systematic way.

Gradually the two cities were uncovered with all the information they contained. Shops have been recognized by the objects found in them; and large quantities of fruits preserved in glass vessels, loaves of bread, molds for pastry, fishing-nets, and many other objects have been found in such condition as to be easily identifiable. In Pompeii, dyers' shops, a tannery, and a works where pigments and paints were ground and mixed have come to light. The last must have been an important business in a community where almost all the rooms of every house were painted. There is a surgeon's house complete with his bronze instruments. In another part of the town is the workshop of a sculptor containing his tools, together with blocks of marble and partly finished statues.

S ome 1900 years after the obliteration of Pompeii, during the autumn days of 1966, fate again began to creep up on another Italian city. This time the victim of nature's fury was to be Florence, the great city of the Medicis on the River Arno. Far to the north of Florence rain had been falling heavily for days. Between November 3 and 4, eight inches of rain fell in the Arno valley. The Arno grew fat and furious with the feeding torrents.

Flooding was not new to the Florentines. A terrifying swamping on November 4, 1333, had swept away the city's

Above: Among the structures remaining in Pompeii are this bakery and several flour mills.

The wall-paintings of Pompeii —many of them in an excellent state of preservation —tell us a great deal about the lives and tastes of its citizens. This one *(right)* in the Villa of Mysteries shows a boy reading a ritual. The still life *(above)*, now removed from its wall, hangs in the Archaeological Museum in Naples.

two main bridges, the Ponte alla Carraia and the Ponte Santa
Trinità. Lesser onslaughts followed in 1547, 1557, 1740, and
on November 4, 1844. An ominous date, November 4,
because it was that same day in 1966 when the "city of the
lilies," the greatest art center in the world, was hit with a
suddenness that shocked the world.

Earlier floods had been braked by the old city walls, but
these had long since been demolished. Once the river banks
had been surmounted there was now nothing to hold back the
flood. Water laden with mud, sand, gravel, chemicals, in-
describable filth, and a rich topping of dark-brown fuel oil
spurted across the city at speeds of up to 40 miles an hour.
Florence, the once proud center of the Italian Renaissance, and
still the living museum of Italy, was covered with wave upon
wave of slime. In places the muck-laden floodwater reached
a depth of 18 feet. The Bargello was covered to a depth of
10 feet; the Horne Museum—14 feet; Casa Buonarroti—18
feet; Museo dell'Opera di Santa Croce—15 feet.

When the waters began to recede the next day, the tragedy
was all too obvious. Paintings, sculptures, manuscripts—
works of art and craft of every kind—were smothered in mud.
The unique collections of ceramics in the Archaeological
Museum lay shattered in a dirty mire of clay and oil. The
Director knew that to restore the collections to anything like
their former state would entail almost a fresh excavation. But
this excavation would be far more difficult than any of those
by which the exhibits had first been brought to light, because
pieces of Greek, Roman, Cretan, and Etruscan pots were now

Part of the prodigious task of
cleaning up after the floods in
Italy in 1966. Here, students
work along with experts
cleaning mud-soaked books.

all mixed together. Only the highly trained expert could hope to disentangle the appailing puzzle.

It seemed almost as if nothing had escaped. In the Church of Santa Croce, the once magnificent *Crucifixion,* a landmark in the history of art, painted by Giovanni Cimabue in the 1200s, lay face down in the sticky mud. Large areas of its paint were already missing. Everywhere throughout the city marble statues wore hideous drapes of black oil. Many wall paintings were stained and scratched beyond recognition by the swirling, gravel-laden waters. Weapons in the Bargello Museum were already beginning to rust, while intricate inlay work on sword-hilts, shields, and gun-stocks was disintegrating. In the ground floor and basement rooms of libraries, hundreds of thousands of manuscripts and priceless books lay soaking up the thick black scum. Three miles of shelves in the State Archives were submerged. Two hundred thousand books were damaged in the National Library, and the same number were caught in the cellars of the Gabinetto Viesseux and the Palazzo Strozzi.

There was chaos in the restoration laboratory of the Uffizi

A statue of Mary Magdalene, coated with oil during the 1966 Florence flood, is given a shower bath of ether and benzol. The specialist wears a mask for protection.

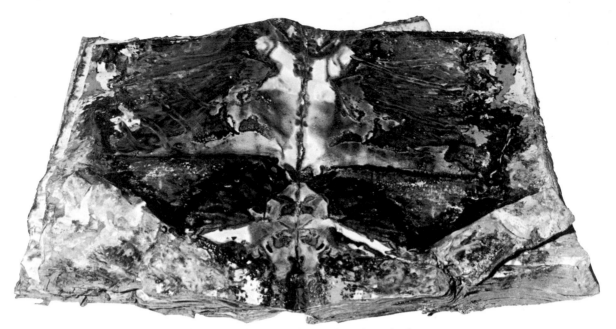

where the floodwaters had swirled around works that had been brought in for restoration. The city, the nation—indeed, the whole world of art—were stunned.

The waves of shock were immediately followed by a warming worldwide response. Because of the urgency of the problem that faced Florence, national and international committees were quickly formed to rush through urgent first-aid measures. Not always, however, with wisdom. Hundreds of soaked paintings were faced with tissue, stuck on, not with a water-soluble adhesive, but with Paralloid, an immensely strong synthetic that was later to need a long soaking with the solvent xylene to remove it. Books were gathered up by the barrowful and in many instances dried with the mess still intact.

The British Museum, one of the many foreign museums to come to the aid of Florence, offered to restore 5,000 volumes. In many cases the books had dried like bricks, with bindings torn off and spines and edges broken. All were in grave danger of attack by molds. They had to be painstakingly moistened, washed, and disinfected. Where fuel oil and other contaminants were detected, specialized cleaning was necessary. To carry out this task correctly each book had to be completely dismembered. After each single page had been treated, it had to be resized, dried out, and finally rebound.

The historic Palazzo Davanzati in Florence became the center of a desperate effort to rescue objects of wood, metal, and marble. In the once splendid rooms of the palazzo, teams of experts from many countries worked together to assess the complicated job in front of them; never had such a vast range of works of art been so extensively damaged. In many cases, the restorers were working blind, because some of the

Above: Attempting to clean a single book is an intimidating prospect when the book is as severely damaged as this one, caught in the Florence flood. Multiplied by thousands of volumes, the job reaches immense proportions—as this scene *(bottom right)* in a Florence library suggests.

Above right: Lines of fine leather book-bindings are festooned across a room in post-flood Florence. These will need careful treatment, not only with leather dressing to bring back their suppleness but also with fungicides to prevent outbreaks of molds.

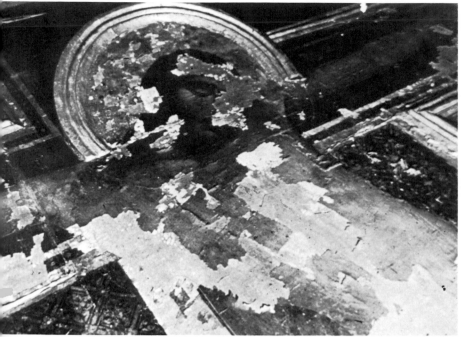

The great Crucifix of Cimabue was one of the tragedies of the Florence floods. Muck-laden waters almost completely wrecked this masterpiece in a few hours, removing not only large areas of paint but also much of the underlying ground.

One of the marble statues left coated with mud by the Florence floodwaters.

problems had never been encountered before. Pooling knowledge and experience, they developed completely new techniques.

In some ways the white Carrara marble, used for statues and decoration all over Florence, was the most difficult. Even in normal circumstances stained marble is notoriously hard to clean. Straightforward application of ordinary cleaners makes the task worse by driving the stain still deeper into the marble. For a while there seemed to be no answer to the baffling problem. Finally Kenneth Hempel, of the Victoria and Albert Museum, worked out a technique that was both simple and effective. He made a paste consisting of a solvent and a soft powdery material called sepiolite, and applied it to the stained marble. As the solvent evaporated, the stain was drawn out of the marble and into the paste, which then fell off.

Behind the main railroad station in Florence is the rambling red-tiled military barracks known as the Fortezza di Basso. Here the picture restorers gathered with their equipment, forming the nucleus of what was eventually to grow into the greatest picture-restoring laboratory in the world. Eighty of the leading specialists from 14 countries combined their skills in a collective effort to save more than 1,200 paintings.

Many of the pictures brought to the Fortezza were already faced with tissues—often in a very makeshift way. Others came direct from the churches, palaces, and galleries. A few had been given some preliminary treatment; most had not.

The restorers first removed facing material and crusts of dried clay and muck. Then paintings on canvas or wood supports were thoroughly examined to see just how far-reaching the damage was. In almost every case, paintings on canvas had to be relined to consolidate the priming and paint layers. Many paintings on wood had to be transferred. One very interesting historical point came out of this examination. Much of the wood was obviously in a worm-eaten state when the artists first painted on it. Even at the height of the Italian Renaissance, artists were poor.

Besides damaging the paint layers and supports, the soaking floodwaters had caused the sizing and the ground of many pictures to swell, resulting in areas of blistering and flaking paint. To deal with this, a wax-resin mixture was gently ironed into the surface of the affected pictures with electrically heated spatulas. This process flattened the blistered paint and ground and caused them to re-adhere to the support.

Cleaning up the aftermath of the Florence disaster is still going on today. The restorers working at the Fortezza estimate that they may not finish their job until well into the 1980s. It is already certain that other groups in and around Florence—particularly those working on books and manu-

scripts—will still be at work in the 1990s, and some forecasts estimate it will take between another 50 and 100 years.

But in a number of cases statues, paintings, manuscripts, and other art treasures are ruined beyond repair. The tragic truth is that not even the skill and dedication of modern experts can undo the effects of their dreadful mutilation.

Although many priceless works are gone forever, the response of restorers throughout the world has made the Florentine disaster—while no less tragic—in some ways beneficial. New techniques and approaches have been tried out for the first time and proven. Lessons have been learned that will benefit future generations of art lovers. Amongst the tragic destruction there is at least an element of hope.

In the crypt of the Church of Santa Croce in Florence, this *Pietà* by Baccio Bandinelli (1493-1560) awaits cleaning after the flood.

An example of one of the "sinopias" or under-drawings that were exposed by the transfer of the frescoes in Florence. These were carried out using a red-ocher pigment with some form of weak binder, and were intended as a guide for the finished fresco.

Florence has probably the finest single collection of *frescoes,* or wall paintings, anywhere in the world. The flood damage to this priceless treasury called for exceptional steps to save the casualties. Principally under the direction of Professor Ugo Procacci, Professor Dino Dini, and Professor Leonetto Tintori, technicians have carried out a rescue operation that actually involved a wholesale transfer of damaged frescoes off the walls on which they were painted.

There are two distinct types of fresco, each of which called for a different variant of the rescue operation. True, or *buon,* frescoes are painted on plaster (*intonaco*) that is still damp or fresh (*fresco*). The pigment penetrates the wet plaster and becomes one with it. Wall paintings done by what is called the *secco*, or dry, technique, on hardened plaster, are not frescoes in the strict sense of the word, but require a binding medium such as egg yolk (for tempera paintings) or oil (for oil paintings) to hold the pigments together and to stick them to the wall.

With true fresco, the painter would first compose his picture in outline with charcoal on the underlayer of plaster on the wall. When he was satisfied with the main features, he would complete the drawing with a deep red ocher called *sinopia* (from the place of its origin), and then brush away any remaining charcoal with feathers. As the walls to be painted were often very large, the painter would be unable to cover the whole picture at one sitting. So under his direction, the plasterer would lay in an area of several square feet of intonaco or, upon occasion, a few square yards. It was on this layer of moist plaster that the picture would begin to take shape. Now the painter would be unable to see the sinopia beneath the fresh plaster and would have to remember what was there and be guided by what was still showing.

The first step in the treatment of the flood-damaged frescoes was to remove them completely from the walls. There are two methods for doing this. The first is known as *distacco*, and is only used where the *buon* or true fresco is well preserved, with the pigments and plaster firm. With this method both the color layer and the plaster are removed together in a single piece. The second method is the *strappo*, which removes only the paint layers by pulling them from the *intonaco*. It was the *strappo* technique which was used for most of the frescoes and sinopias that were rescued in Florence.

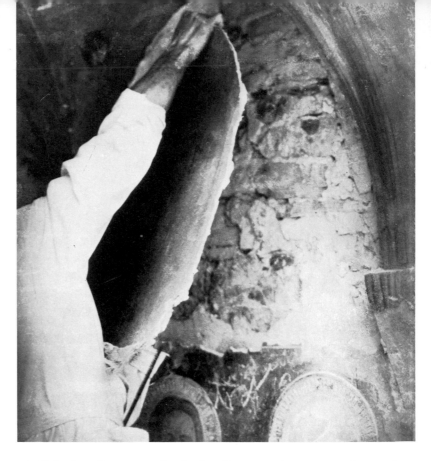

Removing a fresco by the *distacco* method. Having applied two layers of cotton canvas to the fresco, using a soluble animal glue, the specialist taps the entire surface of the painting with a rubber hammer, and then removes the painting, along with the underlying plaster.

With the *distacco* method, the first step is to treat the surface of the fresco with a dilute acrylic fixative to form a clear protective coat. Then two layers of cotton canvas are glued over the whole picture with a soluble animal glue with just a little molasses added for flexibility. When this is dry, the canvas-covered painting is tapped all over with a rubber mallet. Then the seemingly impossible suddenly becomes possible. The whole painted *intonaco* layer and canvas can be levered from the under layer of plaster by using long steel knives.

The whole fresco is then laid face down on a flat support and the rough plaster on the back smoothed down. The final thickness of the canvas and plaster sandwich may be about one half inch. Next it is attached to a fresh support which is generally two pieces of masonite glued together. A second method is to use a sandwich of fiber glass, plastic foam, and plaster board. The whole is then left to harden for two or three weeks. Lastly, the facing canvas is taken off with hot water and steam jets. If cleaning is needed this is done with plentiful supplies of water or, in obstinate cases, with a solution of ammonia.

The *strappo* method again calls for a facing with canvas, which is once more applied with animal glue, but this time generally with no molasses. When the facing canvas has dried on, it is literally ripped from the bottom upward in a sudden steady pull, and, miraculously, the whole paint layer comes away from the wall. The picture is then remounted onto a rigid support, using an adhesive of acrylic solution with calcium carbonate.

In the first 18 months of intricate and extremely demanding work, some 25,000 square feet of frescoes were saved by dedicated and skilled restorers.

The tragedy at Florence and the work that followed spotlighted the continuing need to save the masterpieces there. Much publicity has also been centered on Venice. The island city at the head of the Adriatic Sea seems at last to be giving up the unequal battle to stay afloat. Originally built as a refuge for the inhabitants of the mainland plains when they fled from the barbarians, Venice can trace its history back to A.D. 452; but it was not until 568 that the first corporate community was formed. It spread over 12 townships on various islands, of which Rialto, now Venice, was the most important.

The earliest art of Venice was Byzantine. Her masons, mosaicists, and glassworkers have become world-famous. Her celebrated painter sons include the Bellinis, Titian, and Tintoretto. During the 15th century the printing presses of the city produced more books than those of Rome, Milan, Naples, and Florence combined.

Today the somber fact is that Venice, the jewel city of the Adriatic, is sinking on an average one inch in five years. It does not take much of a head for mathematics to work out how long it will be before the city will be abandoned—if nothing is done.

Venice caught it badly the same day as Florence did in 1966. The severe storm all over the north of Italy was joined on the Adriatic coast by three days of wind, the vicious *sirocco*, which brought a high tide six feet above normal. The resultant disastrous damage of the flood that lasted 20 hours awoke the world to the unique problems of Venice, which offers restorers their greatest challenge ever. An Institute has been set up in Venice where scientists—geologists, oceanographers, meteorologists, physicists, chemists, and engineers—are collecting data. Their first task is the actual physical conservation of the city. Computers are analyzing tide movements, the wave patterns, flood cycles, and the drop of the fresh water table—that is, the layer of fresh water beneath the city resulting from ever-increasing pumping from artesian wells. This is restoration on a fantastic scale, and although it will eventually cost millions and millions of dollars the basic techniques are the same as for any restoration job.

The archaeologist has shown in many places how the unbridled fury of ancient warring peoples razed cities to the very foundations, the victor seeking to expunge all

traces of the loser's culture. Unhappily, throughout history, war has continually gouged away our precious store of works of art and architecture. When aided by the destructive fury of inflamed rioters the effect can be catastrophic.

In the 16th century a wave of fanaticism swept across the Low Countries—Holland and Belgium. In a history of the Rebellion of the Netherlands, Friedrich Schiller describes the scene of August 1566 when gangs of beggars, peasants, sailors, and workmen burst into churches with the single purpose of destroying works of art they associated with idolatry. Antwerp's churches suffered harshly. Carved woodwork was hacked to pieces with axes, paintings destroyed or spoiled, organs wrecked, gold and silver plate stolen and melted down. In Holland, cities had the choice of taking the offending works of art from their churches or having the mob unleashed to continue the desecration.

Here a French restorer is working on a very large panel in the Fortezza di Basso in Florence. She is lying on a foam mattress placed on a wooden gantry over the picture, and is carefully replacing fragments of dislodged paint.

Nearly 400 years later, another wave of destruction was launched against art. As part of the supernationalist Nazi propaganda, Hitler declared that there must be a return to classic beauty, and he denigrated all art since Impressionism as symbols of decadence and weakness. To further his aim, exhibitions of modern art organized under the heading of Chambers of Horror of Art were shown in the major cities of Germany.

In 1937, the year after the Olympic Games, Hitler ordered Goebbels to remove from the museums and galleries of the country all of the art officially labeled "the work of German decadent art since 1910." But in the frenzy of rising Nazi spleen this definition became blurred—very little attention was paid to the nationality of painters or their dates. As a result, works by a great many leading European artists, including Munch, Van Gogh, Gauguin, Manet, and Cézanne,

Venice, always under siege from the waters of the Adriatic, suffered badly during the floods.

were named. In a vast warehouse in Berlin, Hitler's art experts accumulated 1,290 paintings, 7,350 watercolors, drawings, and prints, and 160 pieces of sculpture, all raided from the nation's museums. Although the Nazis may have been mad, they were not stupid. Much of the "decadent art" was sold at a great sale in Lucerne, Switzerland. To complete the rape of the great German collections, the Nazis built a bonfire in the courtyard of the main fire station in Berlin and consigned to the flames about 1,000 oil paintings and nearly 4,000 watercolors, drawings, and prints.

During the Second World War, movable works of art escaped damage to some degree, because the countries of Europe, knowing what was coming, took them to places of safety. Architecture, however, took a savage battering. In the medieval city of Danzig the whole area of the Old Water Front was ruined, and so was the Arsenal, which was one of the finest examples of Renaissance brick building in Northern Europe. In Kiev, the Perchersk Lavra Monastery or Monastery of the Catacombs, was completely destroyed. This was one of the most sacred places in Russia, where the relics of the early Russian saints were stored.

Aerial bombardment wrecked the Dutch Church in London that was given in 1550 by Edward VI to Protestant refugees from the Continent. In Italy, the Monastery of Cassino, founded by Saint Benedict in 529, was caught between the armies and slowly crunched to pieces by the combined forces of opposing artillery. The story of the savaging of Europe's architectural heritage fills many volumes, for modern weapons are lethal not only to people but also to great buildings.

Fortunately, in many places archives that could show exactly what many of these buildings were like had been preserved. And so all over Europe the restorers are working to salve the wounds of war. In Leningrad, the Winter Palace and the Admiralty are now nearly completely restored. In Münster, Germany, the Gothic Town Hall built in 1335 has been raised again from the rubble.

The world is fast waking to the value of the services of those trained in restoration and conservation. In Rome the International Center for the Study of the Preservation and Restoration of Cultural Properties serves all countries by helping to train student restorers and providing up-to-date information on techniques and equipment. Some of its experts have worked with UNESCO restoring Buddhist temples in South Korea, while others have conserved early cave paintings in India. Help has been given to save frescoes on the Mayan site of Bonampak in Mexico, and also to assist in restoration of the ancient painted dome structures at Kassanluk in Bulgaria.

Humans have played a big part in the destruction of art, and World War II saw destruction carried to new lengths. The pictures below show the effect of Allied bombing on the architecture of Cologne, Germany, and the rubble of the High Altar of St. Paul's Cathedral, London, after an attack by German bombers.

The headquarters of the International Institute for the Conservation of Historic and Artistic Works, which has members all over the world, is located in London. Under its aegis ideas and profits from experience are exchanged. Its periodicals document the advances that come from the work of members. Thus there is hope that in art, as in all human effort, international cooperation may preserve some of the treasure of our human heritage as a record and inspiration for generations to come.

A Look at the Past

The word "museum," is derived from the Greek "mouseion," which, literally translated, means a sanctuary for the muses of ancient mythology. They were the nine goddesses who held sway over the arts and sciences. In the early Greek period the study and the practice of the liberal arts was very much an essential for everyone, more so even, perhaps, than today. The arts, the work of human hands, have been seen by philosophers of all periods as an escape, a refuge from materialism.

The interior of an art gallery, a detail from a painting by an anonymous artist of the Flemish school of the early 1600s. Increased affluence in Europe at this period led to a greater demand for paintings, and they began to be regarded as status symbols.

The first establishment to be called a museum was not in the modern sense one at all. The museum that was built in 280 B.C. by Ptolemy Soter, ruler of Alexandria, Egypt's chief city at that time, was more in the nature of a school or university. Located in the heart of Alexandria, Ptolemy's museum contained, apart from the famous library, a whole complex of departments for the use of students and scholars. Among them were a zoo, a garden of rare plants, and rooms for research into such sciences as anatomy and astronomy.

Oxford's Ashmolean Museum, founded by Elias Ashmole 300 years ago, houses one of the world's outstanding Natural History collections.

In the second century B.C. a Greek writer described a building on the Acropolis at Athens that contained a hall called the Pinakotheke, which had paintings on public display. The hall's name survives today with the famous gallery in Germany, the Munich Pinakothek. In the territory of modern Turkey there was an ancient empire of Pergamum, which was ruled over by a dynasty of Hellenistic kings (283-133 B.C.) called Attalids. The dynasty was founded by Philetaeros and named after his nephew, King Attalus, who extended the empire to its broadest reaches around 240 B.C. The kings of Pergamum gathered and displayed quantities of sculpture, paintings, books, precious jewels, and other objects. When they could not obtain the originals, they had copies made. There was also a rudimentary catalog of the objects.

The Attalids were not the only collectors of the ancient world. Hanno, after his voyage to the West Coast of Africa, gave some female gorilla skins to be hung in the temple of Astarte in Carthage. Alexander the Great not only supplied large sums of money to Aristotle for scientific researches, but

The Grand Gallery of the Louvre in Paris, in the mid-19th century, filled with art students copying the works of the old masters.

also sent him natural history collections from those countries he conquered. Further, he put thousands of men at Aristotle's service to collect specimens.

In later centuries, when the Roman legions marched across Europe, the near Middle East, and North Africa, they not only conquered but also plundered. The art of a city or country gave it a prestige that others sought to acquire, and the returning armies brought back to Rome treasures from all over the Empire. The collections of Greece filled the great galleys that were pulled back to Italy by sweating slaves. The imperial Romans became passionate collectors of foreign art. Many of the rich added galleries to their villas and adorned their homes not only with works of art, but also with strange objects of natural history brought back by soldiers and travelers.

Marcus Agrippa (63-12 B.C.), the son-in-law and adviser of the Emperor Augustus, lamented that too many wealthy Romans were removing their treasures to their private villas, and urged that pictures, statues, and valuable artifacts should be made accessible to all. This is the first recorded statement of the value of an art collection as a cultural heritage, and of the general public's right to enjoy it. A popular architect of the early Empire named Vitruvius gave some advice on the display of art, which in basic principles is relevant today. He recommended that galleries for paintings face north "because the light is the same at every hour, and therefore the colors always remain constant." Libraries, he said, should face east

This example of early medieval artistry, *The Grotto of the Virgin*, is one of the treasures of St. Mark's Cathedral in Venice. The rock crystal vase encloses a bronze statuette of the Virgin and is mounted on the crown of the Byzantine Emperor Leo VI (886-912).

Opposite, above: The British Museum, London, in the 1800s. *Below*: During this period, the British Museum still housed a Natural History collection, which was very popular with the visitors.

"because their use demands morning light." He explained that south and west exposures were unsuitable for both galleries and libraries as such positions were "subject to the humidity of the winds," and "encourage worms and the growth of molds."

When the great Academy at Alexandria was burned in 640 by the Arabs, probably at the orders of the fanatical Calif Omar, the term "museum" and, indeed, the whole concept of a public sharing of art, died. The Dark Ages closed in on educational and intellectual activities. This period of the Middle Ages lasted from the death of Charlemagne in 814 until about 1000.

The medieval Church, however, became a sort of museum, providing a center for various forms of artistic production. Artists and craftsmen worked, often anonymously, to decorate and beautify the great church buildings inside and out. Besides paintings and sculpture, donors also provided exquisite illuminated manuscripts, vestments, gold and silver plate, and crucifixes. Collections of medieval church art can be seen in the Abbey of St. Denis near Paris, St. Mark's Cathedral in Venice, and at the Vatican in Rome. And, of course, the highest expression of medieval art can be found in the great stained glass windows of the churches themselves—such as the magnificent windows of Chartres Cathedral.

The late 14th century brought a revival of learning. In Italy especially, the Renaissance flowered. It is still the greatest period of man's creative genius. Artists, musicians, writers, and scientists abounded and brought about a reawakening of interest in the classical Greek ideas. Once again the wealthy began to collect objects of artistic or historic significance. Large amounts of statuary, gems, coins, manuscripts, and medals were assembled in private collections, sometimes together with plants, birds, animals, and minerals gathered by devoted scholars. With many of these accumulations there was no real order or plan for their display, nor were they open to the public. There were, however, some exceptions. In the cathedral at Halle, Germany, Cardinal Albert of Brandenburg, the antagonist of Luther, put on public display a wonderful collection of religious relics in sumptuous cases, with a carefully printed and illustrated catalog.

There remains at least one firsthand account of such private collections. John Ray, an English traveler and writer, stopped at Modena in Northern Italy in the mid-1600s. While he was there he visited the palace of the duke and later wrote that he was impressed by the "cabinet or museum, furnished with a choice of rarities, jewels, ancient and modern *intaglios* (carved precious and semiprecious stones), dried plants pasted upon smooth boards, a petrified human head, a fly

discernible in a piece of amber, and a Chinese calendar written on wooden leaves."

A famous early natural history collector was a German, Georgius Agricola (1495-1555), who has become known as "the father of mineralogy." It was the elector Augustus of Saxony who established the original *Kunst und Naturalien Kammer* (museum of art and nature), which later became the foundation of the museums in Dresden. There was also the Italian naturalist, Andrea Cesalpino (1519-1603), whose collection of plants is still preserved in Florence. In Denmark Ole Worm (1588-1654), a physician after whom the "Wormian bones" of the skull are named, was among the first to study what is today known as the science of pre-historic archaeology.

In the 16th century rich and noble Italians revived the custom of building private, spacious exhibition rooms. Long galleries became an essential part of their palaces. It was probably the architect Sebastiano Serlio (1475-1554) who first suggested the galleries, which were also used for indoor exercise. The best-known long gallery, which is still with us, is that on the top floor of the Uffizi Gallery in Florence. But even in the early 18th century there were still no museums in the present sense of the word. The collections, small and large, were private and served as a basis for the studies of scholars, as status symbols for the rich, for the personal pleasure of the collector, and sometimes for all three.

In 17th-century Britain two men were to play a very significant role in the development of natural history museums, the two John Tradescants, father and son. Both were in the employment of the Duke of Buckingham and later of King Charles I of England. The father died about 1637 and his son, born in 1608, lived on until 1662. John Tradescant the Elder was a traveler, naturalist, and gardener, and

The great hall of the National Coach Museum in Lisbon, Portugal. Assembled here is probably the finest collection of these elaborately decorated vehicles that can be found anywhere in the world.

A corner of one of the main rooms in Schloss Erbach, Germany, showing an excellent collection of armor, for both man and horse. Also to be seen are examples of daggers, swords, and pikes.

probably the author of *A Voiag of Ambasad* (1618), which describes the voyage of Sir Dudley Digges to Archangel, and contains the earliest existing account of Russian plants. His participation in an expedition against Algerian pirates in 1620 gave the writer an opportunity to collect natural history specimens in North Africa. It was John the Elder who established a garden of medical plants at Lambeth, London. In 1656 John the Younger published a lengthy description of his father's collection, and also his own, under the title *Museum Tradescantianum*.

John the Younger willed the collections, which were reputed to consist of "twelve cartloads of curiosities" gathered mainly from Virginia and Algiers, to Elias Ashmole. Ashmole, after a long legal argument with the widow of the Younger Tradescant, gave the whole collection to Oxford University on the condition that they provide suitable housing. A new building was erected between 1679 and 1683 to plans by T. Wood, whose work was influenced by Sir Christopher Wren, the architect of St. Paul's Cathedral in London. Ashmole wrote in his diary on February 17, 1683, that "the last load of my rarities was sent to the barge, and this afternoon I relapsed into the gout." Elias Ashmole was himself an antiquary and astrologer who studied physics and mathematics at Brasenose College, Oxford. His museum was to be a model for those that followed.

The most famous English collector of the late 17th century and first half of the 18th century was Sir Hans Sloane (1660-1735). He spent a small fortune building a collection that was as varied as it was huge, containing just about every imaginable kind of exhibit, from paintings to fossils. In all there were about 69,000 items and the whole was estimated to be worth over £80,000, which in current dollar equivalents equals about a quarter of a million dollars. At the time, however, the purchasing power of £80,000 was far greater than it is today, probably ten times as much. Sloane bequeathed the entire assemblage to the British nation, so that these things "tending many ways to the manifestation of the glory of God, the improvement of the arts and sciences, and benefit of mankind, may remain together . . . and that chiefly in and

The Salon of Niobe in the Uffizi Gallery, Florence. One of the greatest art galleries in the world, the Uffizi began its existence as the treasure-house of the powerful Medici family.

about the city of London, where they may, by the great confluence of people, be of most use." There was one condition—Parliament must undertake to pay Sloane's heirs the sum of £20,000.

This Legacy of Sir Hans Sloane was to become the nucleus of the British Museum, and with the addition of the library of George II it was placed in Montague House in the Bloomsbury section of London. Later other famous libraries were added to it. The initial display may seem odd by today's standards. In the entrance hall was a statue of Shakespeare, strange ornaments from a Hindu temple, and the huge skeleton of a hippopotamus.

Although the doors were opened to the public in 1759, the museum was not immediately as accessible as might have been expected. A *Guide Book to the General Contents of the British Museum* (published in 1761) notes, ". . . fifteen persons are allowed to view it in one Company, the Time allotted is two Hours; and when any Number not exceeding fifteen are inclined to see it, they must send a list of their Christian and Sirnames, additions, and places of abode, to the Porter's Lodge, in order to ensure their being entered in the Book; in a few days the respective Tickets will be made out, specifying the Day and Hour in which they are to come, which, on being sent for, are delivered. If by any accident some of the parties are prevented from coming, it is proper they send their Tickets back to the Lodge, as nobody can be admitted with it but themselves. It is to be remarked that the fewer Names there are in a list, the sooner they are likely to be admitted to see it."

The opening of the British Museum coincided with the development of a systematic study of nature. The Linnean Society was founded in 1788 by Sir James Edward Smith in honor of Linnaeus (Carl von Linné 1707-1778), the great Swedish naturalist and founder of the study of modern botany. As scientific discovery gained momentum, the preservation, authentication, and cataloging of specimens became an art rather than the near-jumble it had been. It became the custom for professors and scientists to present to museums and galleries the collections upon which they had been working. In the 19th century museums rapidly multiplied and began to take on the form they have today. Besides being repositories for objects, they became seats of learning and more and more freely available to the public.

Museums devoted to the fine arts were quite as long in reaching their present-day development. Like the natural history and general collections, fine arts museums began as private collections. By the middle of the 15th century the Medici family, a powerful and noble house of bankers and politicians in Florence, gathered together one of the greatest art collections ever. An inventory drawn up in 1465 lists hundreds of medals, cameos, Byzantine icons, Flemish tapestries, and musical instruments, together with vast numbers of statues and paintings. As the power of the Medicis increased, so did their collection and their influence as patrons of the arts.

In the late 1500s, the Medicis commissioned Vasari to design a building to hold their treasures. He produced plans for a gallery that was to become as famous as the collection it held—the Uffizi, Florence. There are few museums in the world of such architectural quality as the Uffizi. Paris has the Louvre; Naples, the Capodimonte; and Berlin, the Charlottenburg. But the Uffizi, though used as government offices by Cosimo I, the Medici who was Duke of Tuscany, was designed exclusively for the display of art. Built between the years 1559 and 1564, this symbol of the Medici family is a very long building with closely placed arches that form one of the finest architectural perspectives in Florence. It stands beside the river Arno between the Palazzo Vecchio and the Palazzo Pitti, which is across the river. A private covered way linked the three buildings. The Uffizi formerly housed the main Florentine government offices before it became a museum.

Francis I, the Medici ruler of Florence and all Tuscany in the late 1500s, placed a number of important works in the Uffizi, including Raphael's *Leo X* (the Pope was, by the way, a Medici) and the Etruscan "Chimera" from Arezzo. Among the sculpture found in the Uffizi at the time was much of a famous collection of classical and Renaissance statues that had been used as models by the students of Bertoldo, even by Michelangelo himself. The great collections willed to the Uffizi included that of the della Rovere family from Urbino in 1631. Among other masterpieces in this collection was Piero della Francesca's double portrait of the Duke and Duchess of Montefeltro. A little later, in 1666, Cardinal Carlo de Medici left a number of fine paintings including *The Deposition* by Van der Weyden. In 1675 a collection of Venetian paintings and other art was left to the Uffizi. This gift, which included self-portraits of artists, began the Uffizi's unique collection of artists' portrayals of themselves.

When the house of Hapsburg-Lorraine inherited Tuscany from the Medicis in 1742, a satisfactory order was brought to the gallery. The collections were cataloged and reorganized. It was at this period that Peter Leopold of Lorraine first opened the galleries to the public, and the history of the Uffizi as a true museum and gallery began. With the unification of Italy in 1870 much of the sculpture in the Uffizi was removed to the newly established museum of sculpture at the Bargello Palace and also to an archaeological museum. From that time the Uffizi has been primarily a picture gallery with just a few select examples of sculpture and tapestry. During World War II the Uffizi collection was completely evacuated. At the end of hostilities this gave the museum staff a chance to hang the collection afresh. The pictures had been hung according to regions, but now they are arranged so that influences and interaction between the different schools of art can be seen and understood.

As the Uffizi is to Italy, so the Louvre is to France. The earliest known structure on the present site of the Louvre was a fortress put up by Philip Augustus about 1190. There may have been an even earlier, Frankish, fortification there dating back to the end of the fifth century and the siege of Paris by Clovis. The word "Louvre" may originate from the Saxon word *lower*, which means a fortified house, or from *louveterie*, which means the headquarters of the wolf hunt. Philip Augustus made Paris the royal residence, although in his time the Louvre held little, apart from the crown jewels and treasures. It was then more like the Tower of London, and in size very small compared to today's complex of buildings, which, if we include the Garden of the Tuileries, covers 45 acres along the Right Bank of the River Seine. The first part of the modern structure, the southwest wing, was built in 1541 after the designs of Pierre Lescault. It was Louis XIV who had the main portion of the square put up.

Colbert, Minister of Finance to Louis XIV, spared nothing to help in glorifying Louis, the "Sun King." Culture and the appreciation of the arts became official policy, and among the works of art that poured into the Louvre at this time were many once owned by Charles I, the King of England who was

The model of the Parthenon in the Hall of Casts at the Metropolitan Museum of Art in New York, in 1910. With its details of costumes of the young visitors, the photo is almost an exhibit in itself.

Two of the paintings from the Hermitage collection. *Above*: *Portrait of a Young Man,* by the 17th-century Dutch painter Frans Hals.

Below : *A Game of Bowls,* by the 20th-century French painter Henri Matisse.

beheaded by order of Oliver Cromwell. The Cromwell regime had sold the royal collection partly as a gesture of defiance and partly to raise money. Leading painters were commissioned to decorate the rooms of the Louvre. New wings were added to the Palace of the Tuileries where Louis lived. The façade of the Louvre was finished in 1670, although the work of decorating with sculpture went on until 1678, by which time Louis had moved to Versailles.

Immediately, the Louvre fell into disrepair. Shops were set up in its doorways and many of the large uncompleted sections became dormitories for the poor. In the middle of the 18th century the idea was put forward of turning the Louvre into a public museum. This, however, did not come into being until after the French Revolution. It was the painter Jacques Louis David who was appointed as the first President of the Commission in 1793, the year the buildings were at last opened to the people.

Napoleon did much to swell the collections of the Louvre with looted pictures from Belgium and other works ceded by Italy. After Waterloo, however, the victorious allies saw to it that most of the pillaged works were returned. The Louvre escaped damage during the revolutions of 1830 and 1848, but suffered in 1871 when the Communards set fire to the Tuileries and the Library. Fortunately, soldiers managed to put out the blaze before it reached the main collection.

Possibly the greatest single storehouse of treasure lies in Russia. This is the State Hermitage Museum in Leningrad (previously St. Petersburg), which houses some 2,000,000 exhibits. The museum takes its name from the retreat where Catherine II, also known as Catherine the Great, placed an exhibition in 1765. It was originally regarded as a curiosity room and was accessible to only a few of her close friends. It is even recorded that once when she received a new consignment of pictures she was heard to say to herself, "Only the mice and I can admire all this." The collection was later moved to a pavilion built by the French architect Jean Baptiste de la Motte, and in 1775 was moved again into the Old Hermitage built by Velten next to the Winter Palace. In

The interior of The Hermitage. This sumptuous museum was formerly a palace belonging to the Russian tsars.

1778 another wing was added to the palace by Quarenghi.

Several times in its history the Hermitage collection has been depleted by sales. In 1853 Nicholas I sold 1,219 pictures out of the total of 4,552. In the early 20th century there were private transactions with, among others, Senator Mellon and the oil magnate Gulbenkian. Among the pictures purchased by Mellon were *The Annunciation* by Van Eyck, *Portrait of a Lady* by Rembrandt, and *Le Mezzetin* by Watteau. These subsequently went to the National Gallery of Art in Washington, D.C., along with the bulk of the Mellon collection. The Gulbenkian Foundation's Museum in Lisbon, Portugal, bought *Pallas* and *Portrait of an Old Man,* both by Rembrandt, *Portrait of Hélène Fourment* by Rubens, *Annunciation* by Dirck Bouts, and several works by Francesco Guardi. At about the same time public sales of works from the Hermitage also took place in Berlin and Leipzig. On November 6, 1928, the Lepke Gallery in Berlin offered a catalog that included pictures by such artists as Boucher, Canaletto, Jordaens, Rubens, Teniers, and Tintoretto, and other items including 40 snuff boxes, 47 enamels, 110 pieces of furniture, and 36 pieces of sculpture. The sales produced much-needed hard currency for the financially pressed Soviet government.

The most dramatic moment for the Hermitage must have been in the summer of 1941, when, as the German forces grasped for a stranglehold around Leningrad, the decision was made to evacuate the priceless collection. It was left to the director, Iosif Orbelli, to supervise the mammoth task. Hampered by enemy bombardment and losing much of his staff to the military, Orbelli and his remaining helpers achieved near-miracles. Using up some 50 tons of shavings and three tons of cotton wadding, they packed two long trainloads. The first of these pulled out of the besieged city at dawn on July 1. Drawn by two locomotives, it included an armored car for objects of extreme value, 22 freight cars, four Pullmans, and two flat cars with antiaircraft batteries, carrying in all half a million objects. On July 20 the second train left with 23 freight cars holding 422 boxes containing 700,000 objects. Its destination was secret, but is now known to have been Sverdlovsk, a city on the Asiatic side of the Urals. A third and final trainload was scheduled, but the workers had run out of all packing materials except wooden planks, and the Germans had captured the small station of Mga, closing the last rail link with the mainland of Russia.

Another of Europe's great treasure houses is the Prado in Madrid, Spain. This museum was intended as a natural history museum when Charles III built it in 1785. In 1814, after the Peninsular War, Ferdinand VII moved many of the paintings out of the royal palace and into the then somewhat dilapidated Natural History Museum. Four years later the public museum of art was inaugurated. At first there were only 311 paintings, all by Spanish artists, but by 1850 the collection numbered nearly 2,000 paintings, including works by artists from other countries. In 1868 the collection ceased to be the property of the Royal Family and became a state museum. During this century the Prado has received many important bequests, including the *Virgin and Child* by Rogier van der Weyden, the *Colossus* by Goya, and the *Rest on the Flight into Egypt* by Gerard David. The Prado, however, is for many people the prime place to go to study Spanish painting. There are 32 El Grecos, and Goya is represented by 114 paintings and 480 drawings. Works by Velázquez include *The Surrender of Breda, The Topers, The Maids of Honor, The Spinners,* and the

Below: A collection of Cypriot vases as displayed in the Metropolitan Museum of Art, New York, in 1907. Such traditional, overwhelming displays are gradually being replaced by a more selective, spacious approach—as illustrated by the well-lighted, carefully designed gallery of Greek vases *(right)* in today's Metropolitan Museum.

Portrait of Queen Mariana. Apart from the work of the Spanish school, there is an almost unique collection of seven paintings by the Flemish artist Hieronymus Bosch, among which is one of the most extraordinary examples of surrealism ever painted, a triptych entitled *The Garden of Delights.*

The great museum of the Netherlands is the Rijksmuseum in Amsterdam, which was established during the Napoleonic occupation in 1808. The foundation of the collection was treasures that originally had been accumulated by the Dutch Royal House of Orange. To these were added paintings owned by the city of Amsterdam and the surviving guilds. The collection was first installed in the Royal Palace on the river Dam. In 1815, after the Congress of Vienna, it was moved to its present quarters.

Before World War II Germany had one of the outstanding museum services of any country, and since 1945 there has been much reconstruction as well as new ventures. The Museum of Islamic Art, the only one of its kind in Germany, has been opened in Berlin. Also in Berlin is an ethnological museum, which is one of the largest of its type. It began originally with the art and curio collection of the "Great Elector" Friedrich Wilhelm of Brandenburg.

In Bremen is the Focke Museum, which has, among other exhibits, a large collection devoted to the story of the shipping that has made the town a famous port. The Schiller Museum at Marbach on the Neckar was founded in 1903 and is one of the principal centers for manuscripts, letters, and works of the major German writers. The Cotta Manuscript Collection alone

A gallery in the Pitti Palace, in Florence. The cases hold a collection of objects worked in gold and other precious materials. The flamboyant ceiling and walls are painted in a technique known as *trompe l'oeil* ("deceives the eye"), creating an illusion of solid architectural forms and bodies on a smooth surface.

has over 100,000 letters dating from 1790 to 1900, including 280 by Goethe.

The Deutsches Museum in Munich, which was also founded in 1903, is devoted largely to machines and collections relating to science and technology. Here, visitor participation is invited, as most of the exhibits can be self-operated. The curious can demonstrate for themselves the laws of free fall, centrifugal force, gravity, resonance, and many other scientific principles. The automobile enthusiast can trace the vehicle's development from the first horseless carriage of Carl Benz to the Valier rocket-propelled car. If you are interested in food, there is even a bread museum at Ulm, in Germany.

The oldest museum in the United States is the Charles Town Library Society, which was started in 1773 in Charleston, South Carolina. Another early American collection was made by the painter Charles Willson Peale in 1802; this, however, was soon dispersed. The Peabody Museum of American Archaeology and Ethnology, which is part of Harvard University, is one of the greatest institutions of its kind in America. It was founded by George Peabody (1796-1869), who was born in South Danvers, Massachusetts, the town now called Peabody. He began his career with a dry goods store and moved to London in 1837, where he made a fortune in banking. His generosity

These ship models in the Focke Museum in Bremen, Germany, are part of a collection telling the story of shipping through the ages.

included gifts of more than $750,000 for the London poor and nearly $3,000,000 for blocks of working-class houses in London. He also gave almost $5,000,000 for educational establishments in America.

Three of the most outstanding American museums are the Metropolitan Museum of Art in New York, the Boston Museum of Fine Arts, and the Smithsonian Institution in Washington.

The Metropolitan, which is held by trustees for the benefit of the City of New York, was founded in 1870. It is associated with The Cloisters at Fort Tryon Park, in New York City, which houses an outstanding collection of European medieval art. In its earliest years the Metropolitan had no building of its own, and from 1873 to 1879 it occupied rented quarters such as the Douglas Mansion on 14th Street. During this period plans were made for a permanent building in Central Park, and construction began in 1874 to the designs of the architect Calvert Vaux, one of the planners of Central Park itself. Not many, however, were pleased with the over-ornate structure of Vaux. And it was William Morris Hunt, who had scored a hit with design at the Columbian Exposition at Chicago in 1893, who put forward a plan for a grandiose neo-classical hall that would conceal the older building behind.

The East Sculpture Hall of the National Gallery of Art, in Washington, D.C. This beautiful building houses some of the world's greatest paintings, including a number of Rembrandts and works by Spanish masters.

By 1917 the façade of the "Met" had taken on its familiar look of today. One of the most recent additions has been the Thomas J. Watson Library, which was put up in 1964 to replace the old library wing. Its severity is in marked contrast to the designs of Hunt and Vaux.

The Boston Museum of Fine Arts was also founded in 1870, following a series of attempts to start a public museum. Harvard College wanted an opportunity to make its collection of engravings available to the public. The Massachusetts Institute of Technology did not have sufficient room for its accumulation of architectural casts. The Boston Athenaeum had received a bequest of armor it wanted to put on view. In October, 1869, representatives of these organizations made an appeal to the state legislature, which early in the next year granted the charter for the museum.

In Washington, D.C., is the Smithsonian Institution, which controls one of the largest museum complexes in the world. This institution was based on a bequest by an Englishman, James Smithson, in 1835. There was a minor Senate scandal as to whether the gift should be accepted, and some senators found it humiliating to be patronized by a foreigner. However, the foundation stone was laid in May, 1845. But Smithson's

Two of the world's best-known paintings, *The Birth of Venus* at right, and *Primavera* ("Spring") at left, both by Sandro Botticelli (1444-1510), attract countless visitors to this gallery in the Uffizi.

instruction for his gift—"it is for the increase and diffusion of knowledge among men"—was to cause many years of conflict in the institution's administration. It was first thought that Smithson meant the institution to be a place for academic scholarship alone. Ten years passed before display cases were set up and an orthodox museum setting created. Slowly the initial notions of the Smithsonian as an organization for academics and students gave way to more liberal views.

This brief look at some of the great collections of the world was not intended to be either a complete history of the development of museums or a list of the important ones. Its purpose was to show that museums and galleries are living institutions, intimately connected with all aspects of the societies of which they are part. These institutions not only house the treasures that reveal man's past, they are themselves fascinating records of man's foibles and virtues. Even in so brief an account as this we can see greed and the struggle for power and wealth balanced by generosity, public spirit, and the recognition that, after all, there is something fine about our species, and this must be cherished and saved as a record for all time.

A New Kind of Museum

The heritage preserved in the world's museums does not by any means consist entirely of great works of art. In our own century especially, men everywhere have come to place a growing value on tools, buildings, articles of clothing, and other similarly humble articles that recall bygone ways of life. "Folk museum" is the name given to the many institutions that have sprung up to house such treasures. Museums of this type are invaluable for education and entertainment. Their principal aim is to make the past live again.

Architects, in collaboration with museum and gallery directors, are today producing imaginative and attractive surroundings for displaying the precious and the rare. Above is a room in the National Gallery, Melbourne (photographed in 1969). The atmosphere invites the study and enjoyment of the exhibits.

At Mystic Seaport, Connecticut, graceful sailing ships such as this one recall the seafaring days of the town and help to make it a living museum of a colorful part of America's history.

At Skansen, in Stockholm, Sweden, more than 150 old buildings from all over that northern nation have been re-erected. During the museum's open hours, Skansen's shops and other buildings are inhabited by a staff in the costume of the period. The whole site is developed so as to bring a past era completely to life, so that the visitor can absorb the effect immediately as he strolls among Skansen's buildings and exhibits. From the director's point of view this "walk-through" technique poses many problems. Floors that are tramped over by tens of thousands of feet each year soon need repair and replacement. Iron and steel agricultural tools soon rust in their natural setting of a barn or shed, where they are exposed to the effects of atmosphere. Textiles and leather goods will tend to rot and grow mold. Thus, replicas are used to some extent in folk museum displays.

Most folk or rural crafts museums are comparatively small, much less grand than the 150-building complex at Skansen. At Whitchurch, England, in a single, 500-year-old farm building, implements from the days before mechanized farming bring the bygone days of the English countryside suddenly to life. There is an old hay-baler's hay press and a set of the huge hay knives that were used with it. There is a strange instrument called a balling-gun—a tube that was used to blow pills down the throats of farm animals, perhaps to quiet a horse before its teeth were filed by a vicious looking rasp. Other homely but interesting and increasingly rare items on view are wooden barrel butter churns, cheese presses, and a quaint little three-wheeled milk cart.

In the early 1900s, Dr. John L. Kirk, a country general practitioner in Yorkshire, England, founded one of Britain's early folk museums. Fascinated by the variety of old furniture, farm equipment, and kitchen utensils he came across as he visited the sick in the outlying villages and lonely farms of his moorland practice, Dr. Kirk soon started a collection of the objects, many of which were still in use. He began in a small way, with the brass ornaments used to decorate harnesses and the distinctive metal plates that fire insurance companies issued to policy-holders to nail to the front of their houses for easy identification. (In those days, insurance companies had their own fire engines, which would put out fires only in houses bearing their plates.) As Kirk's enthusiasm grew, his collection expanded, filling outbuildings, his cellar, attic, and any other available space. Because his garage was packed with an old hearse, two fire engines, and a hansom cab, he had to keep his own car in the open.

By 1935 Dr. Kirk's collection had become unmanageable, and he offered it to the City of York. Three years later it was

Shiny, leather-upholstered relics of the days when motoring was a matter of style, not speed, fill this enormous room at the Henry Ford Museum located in Dearborn, Michigan.

housed in the city's unused prison for women. Dr. Kirk was made Honorary Director, and largely through his energy and imagination the Castle Museum, York, was created. Today it gives a lively picture of three centuries of past life in Yorkshire.

The Museum's series of period rooms—many with interiors salvaged from demolished houses and cottages—includes an oak-paneled room of the 1630s, an elegant Georgian room of the 1790s, a moorland cottage interior of the 1850s, and a Victorian parlor of the 1870s. Other galleries specialize in agricultural equipment, musical instruments, and toys. Streets of reconstructed shops climax the visit for the more than 750,000 people who visit York's Castle Museum every year and step back into a part of England's history.

On the eastern seaboard of the United States, a similar but even larger-scale venture is the reconstruction of an 18th-century seaport at Mystic, Connecticut. This imaginative project grew out of a discussion by three men on Christmas Day, 1929. Dr. Charles Stillman, Edward Bradley, and Carl Cutler were all citizens of Mystic, and what they had in mind was a revolutionary kind of museum. During America's early years, Mystic had built ships, and her seamen had sailed all over the world in graceful clippers, schooners, and whalers. When steam-power came, in the mid-1800s, not only the

A bit of England as Dickens might have seen it—a street of reconstructed 19th-century shops in the Castle Museum in the city of York. The museum also includes period rooms, representing life in Yorkshire during the past 300 years.

ships, but also the seaport, began to die. On that Christmas Day the three citizens of Mystic formed the Marine Historical Association, from which Mystic Seaport was to grow again as an imaginative complex of historical buildings, complete in every detail.

Mystic's shops are stacked with goods and products of America's seagoing past. On the shelves of Bringhurst's Apothecary are drugs and medical instruments in common use during the early 1800s, including such gruesome surgical aids as bleeder knives, leech jars, and turnkeys (levers) for extracting teeth. Farther on down the street are sheds and workshops where men are busy carving figureheads just as they were made for the old sailing ships. In a dark, dusty blacksmith's shop, smiths forge hand harpoons identical to those used by the whalers who sailed from the nearby port of New Bedford, Massachusetts. Mystic also has a genuine rope-walk, an old, 250-foot-long shed that was once used for spinning the hempen cables and ropes for the great sailing ships.

A fine library, which holds the records of the Marine Historical Association, has an impressive collection of old nautical journals and logbooks from ships. Here we can read the diary of Albert Burrows, a Mystic lad of 14 who went to sea in 1851 as cabin boy on the whaler *Romulus*.

A woodcarver in Mystic Seaport keeps alive an old craft, producing majestic American eagles and ships' figureheads. The figurehead at left probably adorned a sailing vessel of the 1800s.

A page from Albert's diary reads:
"For dinner each day boiled salt beef and pork assisted each day as follows: Sunday—'duff' flour, water and lard with a few dried apples for the crew and, for the officers, raisins thrown in and boiled with the beef in a canvas bag. Monday—bean soup. Tuesday—boiled rice. Wednesday—pea soup. Thursday—duff again. Friday—no extras. Saturday—salt codfish.

"When there were potatoes or other vegetables on board we had them occasionally besides vinegar once a week and flapjacks every 1,000 barrels of oil. We had flapjacks accordingly three times in the course of the voyage of three years."

But the true pride of Mystic Seaport is the sailing ships that lie at their moorings and alongside the jetties, for, after all, ships are what a port is all about. Workshops, stores, and the people who worked in them were only subsidiary to the business of going to sea and the tall ships themselves. These beautiful relics evoke a time when a sea passage almost always meant hardship. But with all this comes a sense of being a part of one of the most romantic moments in the story of transport. Over 50 of these majestic vessels are to be seen.

Outstanding among the privately originated collections of Americana is the Henry Ford Museum at Dearborn, Michigan. Henry Ford in his lifetime almost singlehandedly revolutionized the American way of life by boosting people out of the horse and buggy era into the age of the mass-produced automobile. Yet, the innovating industrialist had a deep respect for history, and spent millions to assemble a huge collection of everyday items out of the American past and display them in a group of historic buildings. As he said, "I am collecting the history of our people as written into things their hands made and used. A piece of machinery, or anything that is made, is like a book, if you can read it."

Ford began his collection in 1906, filling a room next to his

An example of aboriginal art. It is painted on bark, using red, yellow, and white on a black ground. Shown are two men (one smoking a pipe) in a canoe harpooning dugongs and turtles. Also depicted are two eels, or sea snakes.

own office with the objects he gathered. Today, the Henry Ford Museum is housed in a village containing a collection of American arts and crafts, transport, machinery, power, communications, and lighting.

The inventor of the Model T was among the first to explore the possibilities of a museum that could offer both indoor and outdoor displays. Indoors at Dearborn there are articles such as old-time farm equipment and tools that must be kept under cover to prevent rust and rot. Outdoors, in nearby Greenfield Village, nearly 100 buildings of all kinds have been brought from various states and reconstructed as part of the museum. Ford also set up the Greenfield Village Schools for local young people ranging in level from kindergarten to junior college. The idea was that through these schools, the Museum's collections, and the village buildings, young Americans would learn to understand and appreciate their heritage.

Americans have pioneered yet another way to bring museum collections to the people. In 1936, when the Virginia Museum of Fine Arts opened in Richmond, its charter laid down that it was to "foster the love, progress, and understanding of art and beauty for the people of the state." This presented a problem. How could an art collection in Richmond, the state capital, be a true "state museum," and serve an area of nearly 41,000 square miles? It was not until

Danish Boy Scouts rebuild the old Viking city of Hedeby, which was a thriving seaport until Norwegian invaders burned it to the ground some 900 years ago. The boys—shown here carving out the inside of a boat—use the primitive methods employed by their Viking ancestors.

1953 that the museum staff solved the problem. Led by a particularly imaginative director, Leslie Cheek, Jr., they created a self-contained mobile gallery.

Each of these large vans—there are now four of them—is a rolling museum driven from town to town throughout the state. The aluminium shell of the truck is paneled with cloth-covered plywood walls; floors are rubber-tiled, and the ceilings are fitted with acoustic tiles. A sophisticated burglar alarm system, special lighting, air conditioning, and humidity control make a suitably protective environment for the paintings, sculpture, and other exhibits. Information panels open up along the side of the truck when it is parked. Inside, there are tape-recorded commentaries with suitable music dating from the period in which the exhibition is set.

The first two *Artmobiles*, as they are known, travel the Virginia countryside stopping at scores of villages, towns, and cities. *Artmobile I* changes its exhibit every two years. *Artmobile II* changes every six months. In an average year the two artmobiles travel about 6,000 miles and are visited by more than 75,000 people, almost evenly divided between adults and children.

The two slightly larger vans were added later. *Artmobile III* joins the first two in bringing art to the cities and towns. *Artmobile IV*, the so-called "Collegiate Artmobile," takes exhibits to colleges and schools that have art departments, to provide a focus for programs of lectures. The success of the Virginian venture in providing a museum on wheels has encouraged other states to consider following its lead.

Museum and gallery authorities in many parts of the world are looking for new ways in which to involve the community actively. One of the most dramatic ways of doing this is by involving volunteers in the finding, assembling, and restoring of treasures.

The idea that volunteers should take part in archaeological "digs" is already widely accepted. Probably the most impressive example of this was the excavation between 1963 and 1965 of the rock fortress of Masada in Israel. Thousands of people from Israel and many other countries worked on the dig, paying their own expenses and enduring intense heat and primitive living conditions. Led by Professor Yigael Yadin, the distinguished Israeli archaeologist, they unearthed the remains of Herod's palace, where, in A.D. 73, nearly a thousand Hebrew defenders killed themselves rather than surrender to a besieging Roman army. The amateur diggers discovered mosaics, wall paintings, coins, parchment scrolls, and hundreds of jars containing the remains of food left by the defending garrison.

Local and national history projects that involve the public

The search for the legendary Camelot, the city of King Arthur, which took place at this excavation site near South Cadbury, in Somerset, England caught the public's interest. Young and old people are taking an active part in the many archaeological "digs" now under way in Britain.

can take forms other than organized digs. Artifacts that shed light on the daily life of the past often turn up by a fortunate accident. In the Netherlands, the Zuider Zee drainage project, begun in 1918 and scheduled to be complete in the year 2000, provides a unique source of museum material. This North Sea area has always been a busy shipping lane, and over the centuries numerous wrecks have settled down into mud under the shallow water. Three hundred craft have been discovered, ranging from a Stone-Age dugout canoe to Dutch sailing ships of the 1700s through the 1900s. Nearby, at Ketlhaven, local authorities have provided a large building for displaying the ships, intended as the beginning of a new maritime museum.

Above: This long, narrow gallery is the inside of a van, or "Artmobile," that takes works of art (here, some 18th-century paintings) to people who live far from conventional museums. The Artmobiles are operated by the Virginia Museum of Fine Arts. *Above, right*: The light, airy look prevails in modern museums such as Genoa's Palazzo Bianco. *Right*: An exciting concept using materials and light—the Great Hall at the Victoria Arts Center, Melbourne.

Another example of a do-it-yourself museum, near the present-day border between Denmark and West Germany, is the site of what was once the Viking city of Hedeby. This ancient seaport was an important trading center until it was burned to the ground by Norwegian invaders in about A.D. 1050. Today, Danish Boy Scouts are at work reconstructing the settlement at a point 40 miles north of the original site. The Scouts work in their spare time, as a kind of history research project, to show how Vikings lived their everyday lives. In their enthusiasm for this project, the young Danes insist on using only the primitive methods of their own early ancestors in rebuilding the houses and ships of the original Hedeby.

A museum for the space age. At the Alabama Space and Rocket Center, in Huntsville, visitors can *(above)* inspect some of the rockets used in space exploration, and *(below)* control a "moon landing" of a model rocket on a simulated lunar landscape.

Left: At Shaw Park in St. Louis, Missouri, much use has been made of the ornamental water-gardens to assist in the display of sculpture.

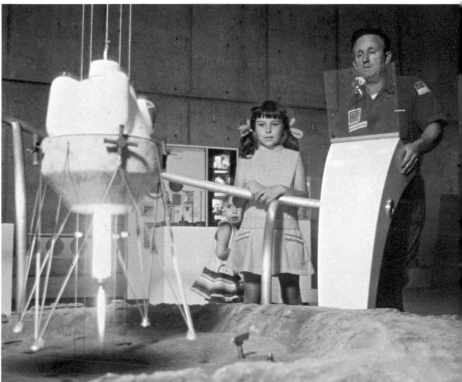

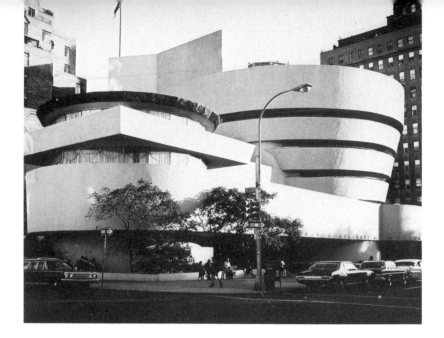

The sculptured shape of the Solomon R. Guggenheim Museum, in New York makes a startling contrast with the neighboring apartment buildings on Fifth Avenue.

One museum that has found a revolutionary way of coming out to meet a new public is the Louvre, in Paris. Having decided that the best way to overcome apathy is to confront people with art in places that they cannot avoid, the Louvre authorities staged an exhibition of reproductions in a subway station near the museum. The time was ripe, for the Louvre Metro stop was being redecorated. Twenty-four works of art were carefully reproduced and, along with photographs of Egyptian and Greek statues, were placed among the gleaming decor of the newly refurnished station. When the station reopened in September 1968, the success was startling. The Metro authorities estimated that there was a 40 percent increase in passengers during the first week. Where before there had been crowds of bored, hurrying people, there were now groups of interested sightseers. Whether or not they were tempted to visit the Louvre itself is not known, but the subway exhibition was an example of a museum involving itself in the everyday life of the public it serves.

In every kind of museum, the heavy showcases, crowded with exhibits and formal classifications of exhibits, are giving way to more lively and exciting methods of display. Sculpture, for example, for long housed in the often constricting atmosphere of galleries, is breaking out of its old environment. Increasingly, planners are placing it against the natural background of a park or a garden. At the Shaw Sculpture Park in St. Louis, Missouri; at the Kröller-Müller Museum at Otterlo, in the Netherlands; and at Louisiana, located on the Danish coast between Copenhagen and Elsinore, sculpture can be seen in the open air against backgrounds of gardens, flowering shrubs and woodlands, and sand-dunes and sea.

In the last few decades leading architects have produced striking and practical designs for art museums. In New York

A spiral-shaped gallery winds around the interior of the Guggenheim. Visitors ride to the top floor in an elevator, then walk down a gentle slope looking at modern paintings hung on the curved walls. A few pieces of sculpture are displayed on the museum's ground floor.

there is the Guggenheim Museum, designed by Frank Lloyd Wright. In Genoa there is Franco Albini's Palazzo Bianco Museum. In Tokyo there is the French architect Le Corbusier's National Museum of Western Art.

In London there is the almost unique example of the Commonwealth Institute, which serves many purposes. It includes display galleries of ethnography, commerce, art, and geography, relating to the different Commonwealth countries, and intended primarily as an educational resource.

Participation is a keynote of some contemporary art exhibitions. At an exhibition held in the Hayward Gallery in London *(right)* people walk among brightly painted planks of wood that they are free to move around as they like. Another room at the Hayward *(bottom)* was filled with circles of stones, creating a feeling of peace and tranquillity.

There is also a fine picture gallery with novel roof lighting.

One of the most exciting developments in the creation of ultramodern museum, gallery, and art center design has come into being in Australia. The National Art Gallery and Cultural Center located in Melbourne, Victoria, will be, when complete, the largest and most comprehensive art and culture center in the Southern Hemisphere. The total cost will be somewhere in excess of $24,000,000, and it will be comparable in size to the Lincoln Center for the Performing Arts in New York. Besides the museum and the gallery buildings there will be a concert hall, a theater, a ballet auditorium, and an experimental hall. The whole complex of buildings will be dominated by a 415-foot, gold-tipped spire.

The revolutionary design of the Center called for revolutionary construction techniques, as the two-and-a-half acre site stands above the course where the River Yarra flowed 40,000 years ago. The bank of the Yarra today is about 200 yards north of the site. The prehistoric river course has become a stratum of mud 90 feet deep, which is subject to tidal influences. Beneath the mud there is solid rock. The plan included surrounding the whole site with a retaining wall of reinforced concrete, eight feet thick, going into the bedrock. To hold the mud back while the retaining wall was under construction, it was frozen and injected with special chemicals.

Museum-goers help to create the exhibit in this 1972 artistic "happening" at Gallery House, part of the Goethe Institute, in London. Visitors sew whatever they like on this huge piece of canvas. The result: embroidered flowers and patterns, mixed with rather crudely sewn messages, such as: "Sew What?"

At Rolandseck, in Germany, an art enthusiast still in his twenties is converting a disused railroad station into a museum and gallery. As the trains are still running along the line that goes through and underneath part of his gallery, he estimates that he will have the biggest attendance of any establishment in the world. For the 12,000,000 passengers a year can see into the galleries as they roar through the station!

A Glossary of Art Terms

Abstract Art An art form (in either painting or sculpture) that relies entirely upon non-natural shapes. One of the earliest painters to work like this was the Russian-born Wassily Kandinsky (1866-1944).

Acrylics Artificial resins that are now being mixed with pigments for painting. They are very durable and allow great freedom for the artist.

Action Painting A technique that involves splashing and dribbling colors on a canvas. The idea is that the unconscious will influence the work. One of the first painters to use this style was Jackson Pollock (1912-1956) from Cody, Wyoming.

Alabaster A variety of gypsum with a fine texture that is usually white and translucent. It is used for carving small figures and ornaments.

Alla Prima A term that applies mainly to pictures painted in oils, it means that they were carried out in one sitting.

Allegorical Pictures Those that tell a story, using images to represent ideas.

Applied Art Artistic work that is added to an object that has already been made. It can apply to architecture, pottery, metal, or woodwork.

Aquatint An etching process that uses areas of tone rather than line. To achieve this a speckled ground of asphaltum or resin is laid on the copper or zinc plate first.

Artist's Proof When an artist produces an etching, an engraving, or a block print of some kind, he normally prints a limited number of proofs. These he signs, and they form what is known as a limited edition of artist's proofs.

Art Nouveau A type of decoration and art that is characterized by the excessive use of curving lines and forms based loosely on plants. It developed in Belgium, France, and Germany at the end of the 19th century.

Back Painting A method of coloring mezzotint prints and fixing them to glass to give the impression that they are actually painted on the glass itself.

Barbizon School A group of realist painters who worked in the small village of Barbizon on the outskirts of the forest of Fontainebleau, France, in the 19th century. They included Jean-Baptiste Corot, Charles - François Daubigny, Jean Millet, and Théodore Rousseau.

Batik A resist process for decorating fabrics, in which the parts that are not to be dyed are impregnated with wax. When the dye has been applied the wax is removed by boiling.

Bauhaus A school started by the German architect Walter Gropius (1883-1969), which worked on the principle that all the art forms (architecture, design, painting, sculpture, and crafts) should be studied together. Teachers included Lyonel Feininger, Wassily Kandinsky, Paul Klee, and László Moholy-Nagy.

Baroque This style prevailed from about 1600 to 1720; it is typified by an extravagant over-decoration that appeared in architecture, furniture, household decoration, painting, and sculpture.

Benin Bronzes Bronze figures that came from Benin in Southern Nigeria. The native craftsmen achieved great skill with the casting process known as *cire perdue* or "lost wax."

Blind Tooling Used in the bookbinding crafts. It means the working of the leather with tools only and without color or gilding.

Block Book Book that was produced early in the 15th century with the text and illustrations cut from the same wood block.

Bloom A misty cloud that appears on some varnishes. It is generally due to the presence of dampness.

Boulle or Buhl Work A decorative inlay using brass, ivory, and tortoiseshell on furniture. It takes its name from the French cabinetmaker who perfected the manner, André Charles Boulle (1642-1732).

Brass Rubbing An impression of an ornamental brass taken by placing a thin sheet of paper over it and rubbing the surface of the paper with a piece of wax mixed with graphite and a dark pigment.

Bronze An alloy of copper and tin. Bronze disease is a disfigurement of powdery green spots. It is generally caused by damp and exposure to chloride salts in the bronze.

Burin A sharp hard steel tool used by an engraver for working on metal.

Cartoon Full-sized drawings prepared for large murals, frescoes, mosaics, stained glass, or enamels.

Chasing The decoration of a metal surface with a small hammer, chisel, and punches.

Chiaroscuro A term used to describe the distribution of light and shade in a picture.

Classic Art An art form in which the artist or craftsman returns to the manner of the

Greeks and Romans between the dates of the fifth century B.C. and the fourth century A.D.

Cloisonné An enameling process in which the colors are separated by divisions of silver or gold. It dates from the sixth century Byzantine period.

Collage A method of picture making in which various materials such as card, paper, textiles, wood shavings, etc., are stuck to the support to give texture or pattern. It started about 1920 when the Surrealists experimented with the manner.

Collector's Mark A special stamp that is impressed on the margin of a print or drawing by the owner.

Coptic Art The art of the early Christians in Egypt from the fourth through the seventh century. It included wall paintings, textiles, and carvings.

Craquelure A descriptive name for the hairline cracks that appear on old oil paintings. These are normally caused by movement, mainly shrinkage, of the paint and varnish films, due to warm or cold drafts, or humidity.

Cubism This was begun by Pablo Picasso and Georges Braque in 1907. Of it Paul Cézanne said, "You must see in nature the cylinder, the sphere, and the cone."

Cuneiform Wedge-shaped character-writing that was developed in ancient Persia and the Middle East.

Cycladic Art Pre-Hellenic art of the Aegean Islands.

Daguerreotype A photographic process that was invented by the French painter Louis Jacques Mandé Daguerre in 1839.

Diptych, Triptych, Polyptych Diptych, a painting done on two panels hinged together, so that they can be folded for traveling. Triptych, one that is made on three hinged panels. Polyptych, an arrangement of hinged panels that has more leaves than a triptych.

Dry-Point A print that is made from a copper or zinc plate in which the design has been scratched with a hard sharp steel point. Sometimes a diamond is used.

Egg Tempera A method of painting in which the colors are mixed with egg yolk.

Electrum An amber-colored alloy of gold and silver. It has been used since the early Egyptian times for making jewelry and for overlaying wood.

Enamel Glass to which metallic oxides have been added to give a variety of colors. It is then fused onto the surface of a metal. The method was used by the early Greeks and Romans. During the Renaissance one of the great centers was at Limoges, in France.

Encaustic One of the oldest methods of painting, in which colors are mixed with hot wax and applied to a surface. They are then driven in with heated irons.

Engraving A print made from either a metal plate or a wooden block, in which the lines have been made with a burin (metal plate), or a graver (wooden block).

Etching A method of printing in which a copper or zinc plate is first covered with a wax and resin ground. Through this ground the design is cut with a needle. The plate is then placed in a bath of acid, which eats out the lines. Printing ink is then dabbed into the lines and the proof taken.

Faience A type of glazed and painted earthenware made at Faenza, in Italy. Now generally applied to other earthenware of the same type.

Fauves A group of painters who worked at the beginning of this century. They liked bright explosive colors. Members included: André Derain, Pierre-Albert Marquet, Henri Matisse, Georges Rouault, and Maurice de Vlaminck.

Foxing Small orange-brown spots that appear as spreading blots on paper. They are generally caused by excessive damp, plus lack of ventilation.

French Polish A high-gloss furniture finish used first in the 19th century. It is made by many applications of shellac dissolved in alcohol and sometimes additions of other resins.

Fugitive Pigments Colors that, from either natural or chemical instabilities, fade or react with and destroy other pigments.

Genre Painting A loose term to describe simple representations of everyday life without imaginative or romantic treatment. It was the Dutch artists of the 16th and 17th centuries who started the fashion.

Gesso A mixture of plaster of Paris, whiting, or some like substance with a glue, which may be rabbit skin.

Glass Painting A technique for painting on the back of sheets of glass. With this the artist has to work his picture backwards, starting with the finishing strokes—for example the highlights in the eyes of a portrait. The colors have great brilliance. The paintings are normally backed with tinfoil.

Glazing This term principally applies to oil painting. It means the laying of thin coats of transparent color over other previously laid pigments. The method produces rich translucent tints.

Gouache A type of watercolor in which all the colors are mixed with an opaque body color. They can be applied thickly, often with textural effects.

Hieroglyphics A kind of writing found on early Egyptian monuments. It consists of characters, some naturalistic, others abstract, which stand for syllables, sounds, words, or groups of words. The ancient Mexicans also used hieroglyphics.

Illumination The decorating of handwritten manuscripts.

Impasto Ridges of paint raised with either a brush or a painting knife to give textural effects.

Impressionists A group of painters who worked in France in the 19th century. The principal members were Claude Monet, Camille Pissarro, and Alfred Sisley. They were primarily concerned with light and used a selection of colors based upon the spectrum, plus white. These they applied with short strokes, which were nearly separated and sometimes completely separated.

Imprimatura A thin undercoat of color applied to a primed canvas before beginning the painting of the picture.

Intonaco The layer of moist plaster upon which the fresco painter will produce his picture.

Lithography A method of printing from a flat surface. The principle is the antagonism of grease and water. The drawing is made with a wax crayon. Then the block is moistened and an oil-based ink is applied. This will stay only on the wax lines. Then the print is taken. The process was developed by Aloys Senefelder, who lived in Bavaria, 1771-1834.

Majolica A type of earthenware with a tin glaze and painted colors which was first made in Italy.

Marquetry A method of decorating furniture by using different colored woods, which are laid on the surface in the manner of a veneer. The term can also include work that uses tortoiseshell, mother of pearl, ivory, bone, and metal.

Mezzotint A method of printing from a copper, zinc, or steel plate, in which the surface is first roughened with a special tool called a rocker. The highlights and half-tones are then scraped or burnished, and engraved lines may be added.

Miniature Painting Pictures of this size generally do not exceed six inches in any one direction. They are painted on small pieces of ivory, parchment, card, metal sheet, glass, and specially prepared porcelain.

Monochrome A picture painted in varying tones of one color.

Monotype A print taken from a plate on which the picture has been freshly painted with a brush and colors. The paper is pressed into the moist paint. Only one print can be obtained from each design—hence the name monotype.

Mosaic A method of decorating floors, walls, and ceilings with pictures built up from small fragments of glass, pottery, stone, and marble set into a special plaster or cement. The technique dates back to the early Greek and Cretan times.

Mughal Art The school of Indian miniature painters that flourished under the Mughal emperors from the 16th until the 18th century. It had a strong Persian influence.

Murals Pictures painted directly onto a wall, as opposed to easel paintings. They may be carried out in fresco, oils, tempera, acrylics, casein, or distemper.

Neo-Classicism A movement in architecture, sculpture, and painting during the last part of the 18th century and the first half of the 19th.

Neolithic Culture The earliest traces in England date from about 2500 B.C. Circular huts were built, weaving practiced, and pottery made. This is the time of the "Beaker Folk." Toward the end of the period bronze came into use.

Niello With this type of work, the design is engraved deeply into silver and then filled with a black composition, usually made of sulfides of lead, silver, and copper.

Oceanic Art Art and craft work from the near-tropical islands of the South Seas. The three main island groups are Melanesia, Micronesia, and Polynesia.

Oleograph A picture that is printed with oil colors to imitate an oil painting.

Ormolu A type of brass especially prepared for castings, which is made from equal parts of copper, zinc, and tin. It generally has a gilt finish fired onto it, the gold being ground to a powder with honey. It was in fashion in France during the 18th and 19th centuries as a decoration for furniture.

Paleolithic Art The polychrome paintings were made during the peak of this period, in about 10.000 B.C.

Palette This may mean the article an artist mixes his colors on, or the colors he chooses to paint with.

Palissy Ware The Frenchman Bernard Palissy (1510-1589) was originally a painter on glass. After lengthy research he finally succeeded in developing the enamel that decorates his ware. Pottery pieces by him often have high relief and incorporate lifelike fish and fruit and plant forms.

Papier Mâché A material for modeling, made from pulped paper mixed with size.

Parchment The treated skin of a goat, calf, or sheep. It is prepared without tanning so that it may be written or painted on. Lime is employed to remove the hair, and then the skin is scraped to smooth the surface.

Parquetry A type of veneer or inlay with woods of the same color, blocks of which are used to build up geometric patterns. The effect is enhanced by getting a contrast in the grains of the woods.

Pastel Very soft crayon used by artists, in which the pigments and filler, such as China clay, are bound together by pressure and very small quantities of casein or gum tragacanth.

Pastiche In a painting it refers to a work in which fragments have been borrowed from the pictures of other artists or produced in a professed imitation of the style of another painter.

Patina A term used to describe the surface finish on objects made from metal, stone, or wood. This may be the effect of age, rubbing, polishing, or weathering, or it may have been applied chemically, as with bronze casts.

Pentimento A reappearance of a design or picture that has been painted over. This "ghosting through" generally occurs with oils. What happens is that the medium acquires a higher refractive index and thus becomes more transparent.

Perspective The law that governs the behavior of lines and planes in a picture to give the illusion of depth and recession.

Pewter An alloy of tin and lead. Its use for making drinking vessels and cooking pots dates from Roman times.

Pinchbeck An alloy of copper and zinc; approximately 80 parts copper to 17 zinc. It was used during the 18th century for making cheap jewelry. When polished it looks like gold. It was named after Christopher Pinchbeck, a London watchmaker.

Plate Mark The impression in the printing-paper made by an etching or engraving plate when it goes through the press.

Pointillism A method of applying small separate spots of pure colors when painting a picture. Mixing on the palette was avoided. It was left for the eye to achieve the illusion. For example, to get green, small dots of blue and yellow would be put close together, and from a short distance away the eye would see the overall effect as green.

Porcelain High-quality earthenware that has a translucent body and carries a transparent glaze.

Post-Impressionism A term to describe French painting that followed Impressionism in the period between 1885 and 1905. It is used to describe the work of such painters as Paul Cézanne, Paul Gaughin, Vincent van Gogh, and Georges Seurat.

Rajput Painting One of the most important phases of Indian Art. In the 16th century artists of this school painted miniatures on paper in a style similar to the Ajanta frescoes, which had been painted in the cave-temples between the first and seventh centuries A.D. The pictures also show Islamic school influence.

Reliquary A small box or casket that can be carried about and is used for holding sacred relics.

Repoussé A technique for producing a design in relief by hammering from the reverse side. It is used in metalwork with silver, pewter, or similar metals.

Rococo A fashion in the arts, particularly architecture, which flourished in Europe from about 1735 until 1765. It means, roughly, decoration for decoration's sake.

Runes Characters used for writing in the Scandinavian and Teutonic cultures. The oldest runic alphabet had 24 signs. The writing probably dates from the fifth century A.D.

Serigraphy Silk screen printing. A form of stencilling that uses a silk screen to hold the stencils.

Sgraffito To cut or scratch back through layers of paint to expose undercoats.

Silver Point A drawing technique that was popular in the 15th and 16th centuries in Italy and Northern Europe. The drawing instrument had a silver point. Exposure to the air oxidizes the faint traces of silver and leaves a dark-toned warm line.

Surrealism A 20th-century arts movement, the title for which is said to have been coined in 1924 by French poet and critic André Breton. It draws upon dream images and subconscious mental activity.

Terra Cotta A term derived from the Italian "baked earth." It can be loosely applied to any object made from clay that has been fired.

Index

Picture Credits

Jacket	Photo Mauro Pucciarelli, Rome
2–3	Photo Mauro Pucciarelli, Rome
6–7	Adam Woolfitt/Susan Griggs Agency
8	(T) The National Gallery/ Photo Stokes © Aldus Books
8–9	(B) Feilden + Mawson, Norwich
10	(T) Courtauld Institute of Art, London
10	(B) Victoria & Albert Museum, London/Photo John Webb © Aldus Books
11	(T) Victoria & Albert Museum, London
12	City of Coventry (Libraries, Arts and Leisure Committee)
13	the Author
14	British Museum/Photo Mike Busselle © Aldus Books
15	British Museum
16	(T) Courtesy Sinclair-Koppers Company, Pittsburgh
16	(B) Photo Dr. N. Stolow, National Conservation Research Laboratory, The National Gallery of Canada, Ottawa
17	Arts Graphiques de la Cité, Paris
19	the author
21	UPI
22	Agence Top, Paris
24	British Museum
25	The National Gallery
26	the author
27	Agence Top, Paris
28	Kodak Limited
29	© A.C.L. Bruxelles
30	Agence Top, Paris
31	(T) Mellon Institute, Carnegie-Mellon University, Pittsburgh
31	(B) Agence Top, Paris
32–3	Musée du Louvre, Paris
34	The National Gallery
35	The National Gallery
36–7	Photos Geoffrey Drury © Aldus Books
38	Michael Holford Library
39	de Sazo from Rapho
40	National Physical Laboratory, Teddington/Photo British Crown copyright reserved
41	(B) Photo Michael Holford © Aldus Books
42	N. Hawley, Research Laboratory for Archaeology, Oxford University
43	Courtesy of Carnegie Institution
44	Carnegie Institution/artist Rudolph Britto © Aldus Books
45	Mansell Collection
46–7	The National Gallery
48–9	the author
50	(T) (BR) British Museum
50	(BL) Michael Holford Library
52–3	(T) Courtesy of The Corning Museum of Glass
52	(BL) John Allegro
52	(BR) Keystone
54	(T) *Observer*/Transworld
54	(B) the author
55	*Observer*/Transworld
57	the author
58	Courtesy Statens Sjö-historiska Museum, Stockholm
60–1	British Museum
60–3	The National Gallery
64–5	the author
67	Michael Holford Library
68	The Metropolitan Museum of Art, New York
69	(TR) British Museum
69	(B) © A.C.L. Bruxelles
70–1	The Trustees of The Lady Lever Art Gallery, Port Sunlight
72	the author
73	Artist Nigel Talbot © Aldus Books
74	Mrs. Enid Moore/Photo John Webb © Aldus Books
76	the author
77	Ullstein GmbH, Berlin
79	Reproduced by gracious permission of Her Majesty the Queen
81	(L) Ehrenwirth Verlag, GmbH, München
81	(R) Victoria & Albert Museum, London
82	(T) *Sunday Times* Color Library
85	Alte Pinakothek, München
86	(B) Staatliche Museen Preussischer Kulturbesitz – Skulpturenabteilung – Berlin-Dahlem
87	Courtauld Institute of Art, London
88	The Metropolitan Museum of Art, Fletcher Fund, 1923

Pictures acknowledged to both British Museum and The National Gallery are reproduced by permission of their respective Trustees.